The K-12 Literacy Leadership Fieldbook

The K-12 Literacy Leadership Fieldbook

Rosemarye T. Taylor

Glenda A. Gunter

CORWIN PRESS
A SAGE Publications Company
Thousand Oaks, California

For information:

Corwin Press
A Sage Publications Company
2455 Teller Road
Thousand Oaks, California 91320
www.corwinpress.com

Sage Publications Ltd.
1 Oliver's Yard
55 City Road
London EC1Y 1SP
United Kingdom

Sage Publications India Pvt. Ltd.
B-42, Panchsheel Enclave
Post Box 4109
New Delhi 110 017 India

Printed in the United States of America

Library of Congress Cataloging-in-Publication Data

Taylor, Rosemarye, 1950-
The K-12 literacy leadership fieldbook/Rosemarye T. Taylor, Glenda A. Gunter.
p. cm.
Includes bibliographical references and index.
ISBN 978-1-4129-1750-6 (cloth)—ISBN 978-1-4129-1751-3 (pbk.)
1. Language arts (Elementary)—United States. 2. Languages arts (Secondary)—United States. 3. Educational leadership—United Stades. I. Gunter, Glenda A. II. Title.
LB1576.T355 2006
428.4'071—dc22 2005003093

This book is printed on acid-free paper.

08 09 10 9 8 7 6 5 4 3 2

Acquisitions Editor: Elizabeth Brenkus
Editorial Assistant: Candice L. Ling
Production Editor: Beth A. Bernstein
Copy Editor: Catherine M. Chilton
Typesetter: C&M Digitals (P) Ltd.
Proofreader: Jamie Robinson
Indexer: Molly Hall
Cover Designer: Michael Dubowe

Contents

Preface

The K–12 Literacy Leadership Fieldbook has been created in response to requests made by principals, teacher leaders, and school district leaders to have a step-by-step approach to developing a fail-safe literacy system. As my friends and colleagues reflect with me on both leadership and literacy texts, they comment that all are helpful in creating a mental model of leadership, literacy, and improving student achievement. These leaders want to know exactly what to do to get there. The *Fieldbook* is intended to create a mental model of what research-based literacy learning looks like in classrooms and schools and at the same time provide leadership with steps to take to get there. The end result is not purchases and accountability plans (which end up dust covered, on shelves), but a living synergistic system in which all the components work seamlessly together. Fail-safe literacy systems can be observed at work every day in classrooms and schools, bringing joy to students, teachers, administrators, and parents alike as they observe literacy learning taking place.

Coincidentally, during the final writing of this manuscript, Dale Moxley, Director of 6-12 Curriculum and Instruction in Lake County, Florida, forwarded an e-mail to me and said, "I had to share this with you. I think this is what we are all about." See what you think:

> I have been meeting with small groups of teachers (8–10) after school. I gave a 2-hour workshop on vocabulary, and we have read *Teaching Reading in the Content Areas* and *I Read It, But I Don't Get It*. During the discussion on Wednesday teachers were so excited about reading in their classrooms, and what they were doing to teach vocabulary better and the effect it had on comprehension. The conversation was so amazing I just sat back and listened. They were making reference to *Just Read, Lake!* [the district's fail-safe literacy system] and how the students were responding better when being taught these strategies.

> Wow! Something is happening here! I love my faculty at Oak Park; they are so receptive to me and what I am doing. I have tried for a year to be friend, resource, and a teacher of reading for them. Many times you have to wait for the payoff and that time has come. I have at least one teacher a day come to my office and share something they have tried with students and how the students responded. I have always thought they were at least trying to accept this "reading stuff," but Wednesday made me realize many are doing it. I can't wait to see what will happen next year!
>
> —Linda Bradley
> *Literacy Coach, Oak Park Middle School*

There are many literacy coaches, principals, superintendents, and others who are positively changing the lives of students through fail-safe literacy leadership. We invite you to join us on this journey, developing a fail-safe literacy system that will result in joyful, independent readers, writers, and content learners.

ACKNOWLEDGMENTS

Acknowledging all of those who have contributed to fail-safe literacy learning—superintendents, principals, teachers, and literacy coaches—would be impossible, but there are heroes and heroines whose commitment to all students being joyful, independent readers, writers, and content learners is deserving of special recognition. To those friends and colleagues: We offer you our utmost respect, recognition, and support. Without you, *The K–12 Literacy Leadership Fieldbook* would not reflect the real practice in schools and districts that is resulting in measurable improvements in learning.

Carmine Arnold
Director of Elementary Education
Lake County Schools, Florida

Brennan Asplen
Principal
Millennium Middle School
Seminole County Schools, Florida

Linda Bradley
Reading Coach
Oak Park Middle School
Lake County Schools, Florida

Francis Catalon
Former Principal
Crispus Attucks Middle School
Houston, Texas

Carl Colton
Principal
Freedom High School
Orange County Public Schools, Florida

Tim Cool
Principal
Stone Middle School
Brevard County Schools, Florida

Debbie Davis
Principal
First United Methodist School
Kissimmee, Florida

Donna Dorio
Reading Language Arts Specialist
St. Lucie County Schools, Florida

Jayne Ellspermann
Principal
West Port Middle School and West Port High School
Marion County Schools, Florida

Brandi Evans
Teacher
Sabal Point Elementary
Seminole County Schools, Florida

Nancy Fuliehan
Learning Resource Specialist
Southwest Middle School
Orange County Schools, Florida

Mike Hurt
Former Principal
Adairsville School
Logan County, Kentucky

Peggy Jones
Principal
Sebastian River High School
Indian River County Schools, Florida

Carlotta Iglesias
Former Principal
Stonewall Jackson Middle School
Orange County Public Schools, Florida

Marshall Kemp
Superintendent
Logan County Schools, Kentucky

Mike Lannon
Superintendent
St. Lucie County Schools, Florida

Erica Massey
Resource Teacher
Mae Eanes Middle School, Mobile, Alabama

Joe Mills
Assistant Principal
Sebastian River High School
Indian River County Schools, Florida

Dale Moxley
Director, 6-12 Curriculum and Instruction
Lake County Schools, Florida

Guadalupe Simpson
Director
LAUSD District C
Los Angeles, California

Pam Saylor
Former Superintendent
Lake County Schools, Florida

David Tucker
Director
Lake County Schools, Florida

Gladys White
Principal
Hungerford Preparatory School
Orange County Public Schools, Florida

Toni Worsham
Language Arts Supervisor
Mobile County Public School System, Alabama

—Rosemarye (Rose) T. Taylor and Glenda A. Gunter

Corwin Press gratefully acknowledges the contributions of the following individuals:

Christi Buell
Principal
Poplar Grove School
Franklin, Tennessee

Jeanine Heil
Director of Instruction, Technology, and
Curriculum Development
Eastampton Township School District
Eastampton, New Jersey

Janet Hurt
Associate Superintendent
Logan County School District
Russellville, Kentucky

Judith Irvin
Professor and Chair
Educational Leadership Department
Florida State University
Tallahassee, Florida

Dale Moxley
Dircctor, 6 12 Curriculum and Instruction
Lake County Schools
Tavares, Florida

About the Authors

Rosemarye T. (Rose) Taylor has a rich background that includes teaching middle school reading and language arts, high school language arts and Spanish at the beginning of her career. She also has served as a middle and high school administrator and a district-level administrator in Georgia and in Florida. In private sector management, she was Director of Professional Development for Scholastic, Inc., New York. Currently, she is Associate Professor of Educational Leadership at the University of Central Florida in Orlando.

Much of her success is due to conceptualizing, creating, and implementing fail-safe systems that work seamlessly to support improvements in student learning. As an example, she led the research, design, and implementation of the Orange County (Florida) Literacy Program that has had its successful impact on thousands of elementary, middle, and high school students and teachers. The classroom concept designed with her leadership has been produced as a literacy intervention product for Grade 4 and up by Scholastic, Inc. In the Orange County Public Schools, Orlando, Florida, she designed and implemented a curriculum system that included curriculum, instruction, assessment, and staff development, supporting the notion that systems make the work of administrators and teachers easier. Through work to support the development and implementation of learning communities to advance student achievement, principals gain structure within which to empower the classroom teachers to make gains day by day.

At the University of Central Florida, Dr. Taylor's specialty is instructional leadership. She has conducted research on leadership, particularly as it relates to accountability. She has given presentations on this topic at the University Council of Educational Administration, American Association of Educational Research, American Association of School Administrators, International Reading Association, Association for Supervision and Curriculum Development (ASCD), National Association of Secondary School Principals, and National Middle School Association conferences. Her articles have been published in journals such as *Kappan, Educational Leadership, Middle School Journal, Schools in the Middle, American Secondary Education, AASA Professor, National Staff Development Journal, Principal Leadership, School Administrator,* and *International Journal of Education Management*. Two books, *Literacy Leadership for Grades 5–12* (ASCD, 2003) and *Leading With Character to Improve Student Achievement* (Character Development Publishers, 2003), reflect her commitment to all students learning more through leadership that creates ethical fail-safe systems. She serves as a consultant on the creation of district and school literacy systems; literacy; small learning communities; curriculum system development; and leadership to schools, districts, and professional organizations such as Phi Delta Kappa and ASCD, as well as with reform projects such as that of the Galef Institute.

Glenda A. Gunter, Associate Professor at the University of Central Florida, has a PhD in Instructional/Educational Technology. She has more than 18 years of experience in education and educational technology, working with schools and educational organizations to integrate technology. She serves as Program Coordinator of a master's degree in educational technology that prepares classroom teachers to apply technological tools to the learning process and to develop the leadership skills necessary for them to become site-based technology facilitators, instructional designers, and technology leaders in pre-kindergarten through twelfth grade schools. She has taught reading to young students and adult nonreaders.

She is a coauthor of *Teachers Discovering Computers: Integrating Technology into the Classroom,* a Web-enhanced textbook, and nine other technology textbooks for Course Technology of Thomson Learning. She has published more than 30 articles and presented at more than 50 international, national, regional, and state conferences. She has received more than $2.6 million in grant funding for education, literacy initiatives, teacher training, and technology integration.

1 Schools and Districts Committing to Fail-Safe Literacy Leadership

ACHIEVING COMMITMENT

"I'm a born again reader!" exclaimed Dave Tucker, principal of East Ridge High School. Principal Tucker went on to share with his faculty that he thought he knew what he needed to know to be a good high school principal until he participated in the district's fail-safe literacy system planning sessions. As a result of his own professional growth in literacy learning, he wanted his entire faculty to become involved in rethinking how they could infuse their daily work with literacy learning so that all of the students would become better readers, writers, and content learners. As he shared his newfound commitment, the athletic coaches at the back table looked at their watches—they had students waiting on them for spring football practice. Then I took the microphone and asked the faculty if they knew why the coaches were present, and the art teacher, vocational-technology teachers, the band director, and the culinary arts chef. Within a few seconds, answers started coming: Because students like their classes, find them meaningful, and listen to these faculty. Yes! These teachers, chefs, directors, and coaches are key to reaching the students who most need support in literacy development and content learning. Next I asked the faculty, "What percentage of your students can independently read your on-grade-level content textbooks?" The answer was about 30%! From that point on, we had substantive discussion from all faculty members, because their value had been sincerely acknowledged and the need was established for each one to learn how to infuse their work with literacy learning so that all students could access their standards-based curriculum. Football practice would have to wait a little while longer.

Fail-safe literacy leadership begins with commitment of the leader to the premise that elementary, middle, and high school students can become joyful, independent readers, writers, and content learners. Without commitment from the principal, teachers who believe their jobs are to teach a standards-based curriculum only will not engage in literacy infusion.

To garner commitment from a diverse faculty, each faculty member needs to acknowledge that literacy is the key to students accessing the content learning for which they are held accountable. They also must be willing to try reasonable strategies that will accelerate content learning and not perceive them as detracting from content learning. Middle and high school teachers are serious about content learning and are open to commitment to literacy infusion once they understand that it benefits the students and the teachers themselves, as professionals. The fail-safe literacy system planning process is grounded in developing the capacity of the school community and creating commitment to continued improvement.

Laying the groundwork to empower all teachers to infuse their work with literacy learning and hence improve reading, writing, and content learning has as its foundation the purpose and result shown in the box.

Groundwork for Literacy Learning Empowerment

Purpose: To create a fail-safe system of literacy so that all students have access to the standards-based curriculum.

Result: All students will become joyful, independent readers, writers, and content learners.

Most middle and high school teachers and administrators buy into the purpose set forth here and the promise of the results. School success is measured by reading, writing, mathematics, and other content learning. With this purpose and result understood, commitment to taking steps to achieve both is an acceptable agenda for most teachers.

Leading for Measurable Improvement

Leadership literature supports four constructs as important for improving student achievement in reading. These constructs are (a) data-driven decision making, (b) a focus on continuous improvement in student achievement, (c) leadership for change and innovation, and (d) shared curriculum focus on standards. Together these leadership constructs provide for the capacity building within a staff and school community that is necessary for long-term improvements.

Data-driven decision making is evidenced when standardized test results are analyzed and shared with faculty, students, and the broader learning community. Studying data beyond standardized test results is imperative and includes looking at data related to the entire school operation prior to making decisions. Leaders who are successful understand the synergistic nature of schools and that each component interacts and influences the others.

Focus on continuous improvement of student achievement implies that a professional learning community exists wherein teachers, parents, and students are always involved in the process of making the school a better place for students. Evidence of a professional learning community includes teachers discussing ways of improving individual and group performance at grade level, department, or team meetings. Shared decision making related to the school schedule and student schedules and to the use of time within and after the school day are common to ensure that learning time is maximized.

Leadership for change and innovation means that teams of teachers work together to solve the school's challenges. Professional growth experiences are encouraged and provided. A risk-free environment exists for trying out innovative practices and action research.

Shared curriculum focus on standards is most likely present in every school, given the era of high stakes accountability that exists today. Alignment of the standards-based curriculum, materials and technology, instruction, assessment, and professional development would be present. Other evidence includes teachers working individually with students to achieve standards, providing more time for students who need it so they can be successful with standards, and professional discussions regarding strategies to meet expectations of standards.

Initial investigation of principal implementation of these constructs suggests that when the focus was on a subset of these constructs, such as *just* data-driven decision making or *just* shared curriculum focus on standards, the gains in student achievement were not predictable. The interaction of leadership that deliberately and purposefully employs all four constructs can, apparently, expect upward growth. Of interest is that these gains in student achievement were not restricted to any demographic area (urban, rural, or suburban), student race (White, African American, or Hispanic), or economic conditions or to the background and experience of the principals (Chanter, 2002; Cupid-McCoy, 2003; Roberts, 2004).

Indicators of each construct can be seen in Accountability Practices of Educational Leaders (APEL), in Appendix A. Some of you may want to take the APEL to see how you score. Better yet, you may want your teachers or leadership team to complete the APEL to provide you with perceptions of others regarding how you incorporate the four constructs. Just as we need to use data to drive decisions regarding student learning, we need to use data to provide us with reflection on how we perform as literacy leaders so we can continuously improve.

Other research supporting the four constructs indicates that principals who are improving student achievement over a three-year period have established literacy as a priority and have adjusted their leadership style to be more data-driven and focused on individual students. As a result of studying disaggregated data on students, these principals are examining their own practices, resulting in

- reallocation of student and adult time at school
- more professional development in literacy learning
- emphasis on personnel selection focused on literacy learning
- scientific research–based selection processes for materials and technology
- refocus of their personal professional time on student learning

These research-based concepts of leadership are echoed in student achievement gains made by the two vignettes that follow and are further discussed as we proceed through the chapters.

Improvements in a Florida Middle School. One such middle school principal is credited with the greatest improvement in the Florida Comprehensive Assessment Test (FCAT) scores in his large school district and has gone from a state-assigned grade of C to an A. On the No Child Left Behind (NCLB) Act of 2001 data assessment, the school also fared well. The school has almost 2000 students, of whom 54% receive free and reduced-fee lunches. It is a Title I school, with approximately 27% African American students, 20% Hispanic students, and 43% White students. To improve student achievement, the lowest level of readers was assigned to a year-long, intensive reading program supported with technology. The time spent in reading for these students was double the remainder of the student population. Additionally, the principal purchased new materials and technology for the students in intensive reading.

Another example of a school using data to make decisions regarding use of time and resources targeted the 25% of the students reading at the lowest levels. After one year, the students achieved a gain of 75% on the FCAT in reading. In addition to these students being placed in an intensive reading class, a schoolwide focus on professional development that would infuse all content classes with literacy took place with the principal taking the lead role, supported by a curriculum resource teacher. Rethinking use of adult time also played a part in this improvement and maximized time for literacy learning. Administrators tutored the lowest readers and promoted vocabulary development via morning school news televised in each classroom. Teachers who had senior interns from the local university and release time during the last portion of the semester tutored the lowest performing students during the release time.

Improvements in a Kentucky Elementary School. Marshall Kemp, superintendent of Logan County Schools, Kentucky, recognized that intervention with the lowest performing Title I elementary school was essential to increasing student achievement. With data available on student achievement over a period of years, this stable community school was selected for the Reading First Grant. As the school evaluated what was working and what was not working in kindergarten through third grade, the data showed that consistent implementation of research-based instruction and assessment was missing. A comprehensive plan of professional development, in-class coaching, new instructional materials and technology, and assessment was implemented. Special education support teachers who previously pulled students out to provide intensive support now go into classrooms to work with those needing intensive intervention. Observation of students, interviews with teachers, and assessment data point to significant improvements in student achievement. This school has implemented a fail-safe literacy system in which the teachers, students, and administrator acknowledge and celebrate the positive changes in students, particularly those who struggle with reading the most.

In each of these cases, the superintendent or principal took the lead to rethink use of adult time, student time, instructional materials and technology, assessment, and/or professional development to achieve content standards through literacy learning. These are key to improving student achievement and are supported by research and practice in schools today. Consider how you establish and demonstrate your priorities with each of these components:

- adult time
- student time
- instructional materials and technology
- professional development
- assessment

FAIL-SAFE LITERACY LEADERSHIP

Freedom High School

The following in-depth description of commitment to literacy learning made in opening Freedom High School in 2003 provides real-life examples of what schools can do in serving challenging student populations. Carl Colton, an elementary principal with a track record of success, was asked to open a new high school that would serve a population diverse both economically and racially. The majority of students were Hispanic and spoke English as a second language. Carl's first commitment was to make sure that all students were successful, so he knew that literacy learning would be essential if that commitment was to have positive results. Therefore he began with his own research and learning about how to infuse literacy into a high school and implement a fail-safe system of literacy. From the initial planning for and selection of the leadership team, including department chairpersons, the promise was made that this high school would focus on literacy infusion.

Personnel

When candidates were interviewed for positions, they were told, "At the new school, instruction at all levels in all classrooms will have active literacy components." Then they were asked these questions:

- How is literacy promoted in your classroom?
- How are reading, writing, and speaking incorporated into your lessons?

These questions led to the opportunity for the interviewer to share the literacy vision for Freedom High School. Interviewees were told that the long-term focus of professional development would be literacy infusion in all content areas, and participation would not be optional. This honest and direct approach allowed some candidates to self-select not to continue the application process and others to get excited about being part of a new vision for serving students.

Creating an Aligned System of Materials and Technology

Selection of textbooks, supplementary materials, hardware, and software was considered appropriate if it was literacy friendly. This meant that the materials selected were respectful of the students and provided support needed by diverse learners, many of whom do not read on grade level. In addition to literacy-friendly textbooks, each teacher would have a classroom library that reflected the content of the courses taught and the diversity of the readers in the classroom.

For students who read at the lowest level, the school opened with two classrooms for intervention. These used *Read 180,* published by Scholastic, Inc. *Read 180* is a balanced approach of software that builds vocabulary, spelling, and fluency, along with classroom libraries for independent reading and teacher materials for small group word study.

All language arts classrooms have *Reading Counts,* software published by Scholastic, Inc. that assesses students' reading levels with the *Scholastic Reading Inventory* (SRI) and provides quizzes on a multitude of reading selections. These products use the Lexile Framework, which provides information on students' independent reading levels and the readability of books so that books for independent reading can be easily matched to students' reading levels and interests. With the SRI in place in all language arts classrooms, an assessment that provides both diagnostic and monitoring data on reading achievement is available for charting student growth in reading.

Media Center

The media specialist was selected for her knowledge of technology and young adult literature. Unlike many secondary school media centers, this one promised to be a hub of activity for the high school students and teachers. In addition to the traditional selections, there were many adolescent picture books, as well as young adult literature, reflecting the commitment to motivate all students to be joyful, independent readers, writers, and content learners. Compact disks (CDs) and audiobooks were included in the selections, providing students with access to on-grade-level literature and content text even if they did not read at that level independently. This portable technology, along with videos and DVDs, supports development of vocabulary, fluency, and comprehension, leading to enhanced content learning. Recent research supports the idea that library-media centers with well-selected materials and technology resources and well-trained librarians and media specialists can increase literacy achievement.

Professional Development

Colton knew that professional development would need to begin with the first person hired and continue throughout the school year. Once the leadership team and department chairpersons were selected, they participated in professional development on literacy infusion. They also attended specific conferences and institutes on the topic. Prior to the school's opening, in late July, the entire faculty participated in day-long seminars on literacy infusion to prepare for instructional planning using the new resources and to support meeting the new expectations. Follow-up sessions took place throughout the school year.

Time for Literacy Learning

As we all know, commitment shows itself in how we spend our time, and that means thoughtful organization of the school day for both students and teachers. Each day during second period, 20 minutes is reserved for silent, sustained reading in all classes.

Ninth grade is a critical time for high school students. Knowing this, the leadership team decided to organize ninth grade students in interdisciplinary teams that were housed together as much as possible to make literacy learning a commitment. The teachers on each of these ninth grade teams have a common planning time to focus on literacy and ensure the success of each student. Furthering this commitment was the assignment of a counselor, whose responsibility was to work solely with identified ninth graders reading below grade level.

Follow-up and Support

All teachers will not be at the same place at the same time with literacy infusion. For teachers to maintain this focus, they must develop their lesson plans using a template that facilitates the use of literacy strategies, the processes of literacy, and reading to and with students to provide access to content standards. Administrators, curriculum specialists, and the reading coach provide support, professional development, encouragement, and feedback.

Stonewall Jackson Middle School

Commitment to literacy learning is also evident at Stonewall Jackson Middle School, which has experienced drastic change in student and teacher populations over the last 20 years. Carlotta Iglesias (since transferred) was an energetic principal fighting every day to provide excellence in learning for her students. More than half of the students come from poverty, and most speak English as a second language. Iglesias was direct with parents, students, and teachers regarding what was expected of them related to many things, but particularly literacy learning. She made a difference in student achievement by enhancing materials and expectations for teachers through professional development and parent workshops. Her approach was to use a research base as background knowledge and to provide appropriate resources first. Then she worked collaboratively to develop a fail-safe literacy system plan. When the planning took place, the collaborative literacy leadership team was well positioned for making informed recommendations.

Professional Development

Monthly, the entire faculty participated in professional development related to infusing literacy into all classes. These professional development workshops took place during planning periods. Although teachers need their planning periods, they found this scheduling convenient. Each session began with an overview of adolescent literacy and the key components of vocabulary, fluency, and comprehension, with the target being access to rigor for all students. Then the teachers shared what strategies they had tried since the last session and celebrated their successes. Next the group developed a scaffold for new learning: They were introduced to new adolescent picture books, young adult literature connected to content standards, or other strategies for improving content learning. To ensure success, new resources were purchased to support content literacy learning, including adolescent picture books, nonfiction, and young adult literature that students and teachers found meaningful.

Four features made these experiences successful.

1. Each one was linked to the previous experience and was not isolated from the overall context.
2. All faculty members participated and were expected to use the strategies in planning for instruction.
3. Administrators attended the sessions with teachers and followed up with them in applying the strategies.
4. Resources (adolescent picture books and adolescent fiction and nonfiction) for teacher use were purchased, and their use was modeled in the professional development session.

These features modeled commitment to the continuous improvement in teacher learning, administrator learning, and student learning. They also speak volumes about how important every teacher is in improving student achievement through literacy learning.

Engaging Parents and Community

There is a profusion of educational literature that supports parental involvement and the relationship of that involvement to student achievement. At the middle and high school levels, we often mistakenly assume that parents do not want to participate at school or that their adolescents will discourage attendance. We may discover that these assumptions are erroneous if we provide a positive culture for participation and create a setting that reflects the needs of the parents. Often parents have had a negative experience at school themselves; parents are intimidated by school personnel; or, in parents' home culture, the role of parents in relation to the school is quite different. If the parents are not proficient in English, they may believe that they can do nothing to help their students at home—but we can teach them otherwise.

At Stonewall Jackson Middle School, a volunteer parent coordinator arranged for parent workshops on a regular basis. These workshops supported the parents in understanding the expectations at Stonewall Jackson Middle School and how parents could assist at home. Because most of the parents work more than one job, just getting to the workshop could be difficult for them. To make it easier, dinner was served for the parents and children who come. One student told me he attended for the pizza and cake, even though he actively participated in reading *Holes* and seemed to enjoy it! Volunteer middle school students provided care for younger siblings so parents could engage in the workshops without distraction.

One particular workshop focused on how to help students at home with reading. About 50 parents and their children (middle school age and younger) attended. The majority of parents requested the presentation in Spanish, so it was provided in both Spanish and English, as were all handouts. Parents were provided with questions they could ask their students each day about content reading and tips for developing reading skills at home. Reading to and with students was modeled with two popular texts: *Holes,* by Louis Sachar, and *Because of Winn Dixie,* by Kate DiCamillo. Before, during, and after reading strategies that parents could use at home were modeled, and the middle school students in the audience participated. Both parents and students enjoyed the workshop and were thrilled that they were given a copy of both books to take home and keep. The next time I saw the students, they asked if I had more books for them!

Mobile County Public School System

Mobile County Public School System is the largest school district in Alabama and has made a commitment to literacy. The system's diversity in race, culture, and poverty challenge the educators serving the 68,000 students. The superintendent has identified improvement in reading as a priority.

In response to her experience as a high school administrator in a challenging school, Toni Worsham, now the Secondary English/Language Arts Supervisor, rose to meet the need to infuse literacy learning into middle and high schools. Middle and high school English and language arts teachers who participated in workshops were motivated with a commonsense approach to infusing literacy based on sound research. Many were excited to learn that their schools would receive young adult literature, nonfiction texts, and adolescent picture books for motivating students and developing vocabulary and concepts as scaffolding for building up to texts.

What is new and innovative about Worsham's approach? Rather than being satisfied with supporting the English and language arts teachers, she knew that real change happens with support from the principal in each school. Because of her excellent relationships with the principals, they agreed to participate in fail-safe literacy leadership workshops to build knowledge of literacy and to learn processes for creating school-based, fail-safe literacy system plans. Teachers look to administrators to provide leadership, set an example, and provide support. Because of Worsham's literacy leadership, all of these were provided to the teachers.

Next on Worsham's agenda was to share the wealth of strategies and materials with other content teachers in middle and high schools. With support from her content counterparts at the district office, fail-safe literacy workshops in the content areas were provided for middle and high school teachers. Participating teachers received classroom libraries appropriate for their class content and students' ages, so they could get started.

At the district level, Worsham's influence is being felt as she thoughtfully designs and implements a consistent approach to improving reading, writing, and content learning in the Mobile County Public School System. This approach includes

- commitment of resources from the top
- workshops for English and language arts and content teachers for Grades 6–12
- workshops and support for principals so that they will be able to design and implement fail-safe literacy systems in their schools
- appropriate, respectful, literacy learning resources related to standards-based curricula for teachers
- literacy materials aligned with content curricula

REVIEW AND REFLECTION

When you reflect on the examples of fail-safe literacy leadership provided in this chapter, how high do you think your commitment is? With the NCLB, we have no choice but to give our best to every student as these fail-safe literacy leaders have.

- Of the four constructs—data-driven decision making, focus on continuous improvement of student achievement, leadership for change and innovation, and shared curriculum focus on standards—which are at the forefront of your priorities?
- Which ones do you need think about and implement more strategically?
- Of the actions taken by these leaders, are there any that you should consider?
- Are there some that you have already incorporated into your school or district?
- What resources, including technology, does your literacy system now include?

Fail-safe literacy leadership means taking risks, setting high expectations, and working hard, as you have seen from these examples, but the research and patterns for success are clear. We will work on them together to build capacity and commitment in the next six chapters.

As you read through the next six chapters, you will be led explicitly in how to create a fail-safe system for your school or district. The examples from schools and figures will make explicit what your work may look like. First you must commit to reading, writing, and content learning for all students. Then a literacy leadership team must be created, as described in Chapter 2. Chapters 2–5 take you through the fail-safe literacy system planning process to develop a fail-safe literacy system unique to your school or district. Because there is a need to enhance literacy learning and accelerate measurable improvement in reading, writing, and content learning, many leaders are turning to technological applications to do so. With this in mind, Chapter 6 is dedicated to technology applications and integration that may become potential solutions or parts of solutions for the literacy learning needs identified in your fail-safe literacy system plan. Chapter 7 addresses how you follow through with communication, evaluation, celebrations, and enhancements to complete the fail-safe system of literacy.

HELPFUL TERMS

Accountability Practices of Educational Leaders (APEL): Instrument that uses the four constructs of data-driven decision making, shared curriculum focus on standards, focus on continuous improvement in achievement, and leadership for change and innovation.

Adolescent picture books: Picture books respectful of adolescents, with on-grade-level vocabulary, content, and language. Beautiful pictures, photos, or diagrams are characteristic of these books.

Audiobooks: Books that are accompanied by cassette tapes or CDs so students can hear while following along with the print. They provide access to on-grade-level content and literature.

Classroom libraries: Collections of texts on various grade levels and in various genres and content and interests areas accessible to students within the classroom. These libraries are part of the fail-safe literacy leadership process that will ensure success and create independent readers, writers, and content learners.

Lexile System: A system for identifying the reading comprehension level of students and of texts.

No Child Left Behind (NCLB) Act of 2001: Reauthorization of the elementary and secondary education act.

Young adult literature: Literature that addresses interests and themes relevant to adolescents.

FURTHER READING AND RESOURCES

Blase, J., & Blase, J. (2001). *Empowering teachers: What successful principals do.* Thousand Oaks, CA: Corwin.

Blase, J., & Blase, J. (2004). *Handbook of instructional leadership: How successful principals promote teaching and learning* (2nd ed.). Thousand Oaks, CA: Corwin.

Brown, J. L., & Moffett, C. A. (1999). *The hero's journey: How educators can transform schools and improve learning.* Alexandria, VA: Association for Supervision and Curriculum Development.

Chanter, C. L. (2002). *The relationship of the accountability practices of elementary school principals to student achievement.* Unpublished doctoral dissertation, University of Central Florida, Orlando.

Collins, J. (2001). *From good to great.* New York: Harper Business.

DiCamillo, K. (2000). *Because of Winn Dixie.* Cambridge, MA: Candlewick Press.

Murphy, J. (2003). *Leadership for literacy: Research-based practice, preK–3.* Thousand Oaks, CA: Corwin.

Sachar, L. (1998). *Holes.* New York: Dell Yearling.

Taylor, R. (2001, October). Steps to literacy: Principal leadership. *NASSP, 2*(2), 33–38.

Taylor, R. (2004, November). Literacy leaders: Improving achievement for all students. *Middle School Journal, 36*(1), 26–31.

Taylor, R. T., & Collins, V. D. (2003). *Literacy leadership for grades 5–12.* Alexandria, VA: Association for Supervision and Curriculum Development.

2 Collaborating Based on Research

Creating faculty buy-in to literacy infusion and to agreement that literacy is everyone's job all day long is necessary because this is not an automatically accepted concept in middle and high schools, as it tends to be in elementary schools. To accelerate the development and implementation of a realistic fail-safe literacy system, schools and districts are encouraged to have a literacy leadership team (LLT). Generally, schools and districts will have some organizational structure that approximates an LLT, but it usually has a different composition and purpose than fail-safe literacy leadership recommends. Most LLTs encountered are made up of English, language arts, and reading teachers. These teachers certainly have a specific role in improving literacy, but they cannot do it alone—or students would already be reading on grade level.

During a conversation with a high school assistant principal about improving reading and student achievement, he proudly told me that this year the principal had budgeted for a literacy coach. After reinforcing what a positive step establishing that position was, I asked if the school had a literacy plan. The assistant principal responded that the literacy coach had developed a plan for improving reading. When I asked, "To what extent have the teachers bought into the literacy coach's plan?" he responded, "Well, you know high school teachers—not much! The faculty sees it as the literacy coach's plan." Although it is a good idea for reading, English, and language arts teachers to have a plan for improving reading, it is a far better idea to have the entire faculty agree to a literacy system, have ownership in the literacy system, and actively implement the literacy system. This can be done with the collaboration of an LLT.

Think about every formal and informal group in the school or district: physical educators, coaches, vocational teachers, media specialists, novice teachers, veteran teachers, content teachers, technology facilitators, curriculum resource teachers, second language teachers, special education teachers, union representatives, and grade-level representatives. If you want the LLT to have real impact, you want each formal and informal group represented. This means the LLT will be diverse in experience, gender, age, race, grades served, and content specialty. Often the teachers who have the greatest influence on students struggling with academic success are the ones never considered, such as coaches, physical education teachers, vocational teachers, art teachers, music teachers, media specialists, Junior ROTC instructors, and technology teachers. To reach all students, it is essential that all teacher groups be represented to ensure widespread consistency when the fail-safe literacy system is implemented.

After organizing the LLT, you will want to assist its members in having an understanding of their purpose: to study scientific, research-based information on literacy and develop a fail-safe literacy system for the school or district. Achieving an understanding of scientifically based research can be painless if it is done by accessing to-the-point publications, such as those published by the Educational Research Service (*Reading at the Middle and High School Levels* and *Helping Struggling Readers at the Elementary and Secondary School Levels*) and *Reading Next: A Vision for Action and Research in Middle and High School Literacy.* Most states offer free online resources like Florida's Online Reading Professional Development (forpd@ orion.itrc.ucf.edu or www.itrc.ucf.edu/forpd), or you may choose to access the expertise of professional organizations, such as the International Reading Association (www.reading.org). By providing the LLT with high-quality professional development that presents research in the context of practical applications to curriculum content and to your teachers and students, you are in a position to plan for consistent implementation of research-based practice across all content areas. *The key to measurable improvement for all students is consistent, research-based practice by all teachers, performed on a daily basis.* To get you started developing a mental model of literacy learning, let's review a synthesis of the literacy research that we find in the No Child Left Behind Act of 2001 and in the fail-safe literacy point of view.

NCLB'S FIVE ELEMENTS OF READING

Before we proceed with the fail-safe literacy point of view, let's establish the background information needed by schools concerned with federal funding and accountability. This includes the meaning of key literacy vocabulary and how this vocabulary relates to all classrooms, pre-kindergarten through twelfth grade. The scientifically based research expected by the NCLB Act identifies five elements as essential for developing good readers:

1. phonics
2. phonemic awareness
3. vocabulary
4. fluency
5. comprehension

We will briefly review these five elements and how they may look in classrooms. Next, we will explore how to be successful with each element by using the fail-safe literacy point of view.

It is expected that when students leave first grade they have mastered phonics (the relationship between letters and written language and sounds) and phonemic awareness (the ability to hear, identify, and manipulate the individual sounds in spoken words). Primary classroom teachers do address fluency, vocabulary, and comprehension, but their most critical tasks are phonics and phonemic awareness instruction, which should be addressed explicitly. Keep in mind that even if a student has measurable improvement in phonics and phonemic awareness, this alone will not ensure that the student becomes a reader; vocabulary, fluency, and comprehension must also be taught. An elementary principal told me recently that the school's goal was for 50% of kindergarteners to leave reading and 100% of first grade students to leave reading.

Although students should have mastered phonics and phonemic awareness by the end of first grade, there may continue to be very low-functioning students at the upper elementary through high school levels who need intensive support or explicit intervention in this area. These students are probably receiving support through special education services, or they may be students for whom English is a second language. Some may even be students with no identified

Figure 2.1 Five Reading Elements

Phonemic awareness	The ability to hear, identify, and manipulate the individual sounds in spoken words. Part of phonological awareness.
Phonics	Understanding the relationship between letters and spoken sounds.
Fluency	Orally reading with appropriate rate, expression, and phrasing.
Vocabulary	Words that lead to effective communication when listening, speaking, reading, and writing.
Comprehension	Understanding the meaning of print.

need except that they have failed to become readers. In either case, immediate intensive reading assistance or intervention should be provided to these students. This may include one-on-one instruction, software, or technology that assesses students' needs and personalizes instruction to target those unique needs. For intervention, software often is more practical than one-on-one instruction by a highly qualified instructor. All schools should have reading intervention as part of their school's fail-safe system of literacy.

Vocabulary

In addition to mastering phonics and phonemic awareness, there are the essential reading components of vocabulary, fluency, and comprehension. *Vocabulary* means the words we must know to communicate when listening, speaking, reading, and writing. Vocabulary may be unique to a particular setting or content classroom and must be deliberately and strategically taught in each class.

From your own experience as a parent or observer of young children, you know that oral language development naturally precedes written language development (we will discuss this more in detail later in the chapter). Therefore it is important to introduce essential vocabulary orally first, with oral practice and associated concrete images that will assist the student in developing mental models of the vocabulary and concepts, as is typical in the early grades. This should be done before students are expected to read and comprehend text with new vocabulary, in all grades up through 12. Upper grade teachers who provide a list of new vocabulary words to be memorized with the definition, then expect students to read text and comprehend, will have less success with content comprehension than those who follow this suggestion. For efficient vocabulary development, think about introducing 5 to 7 new words at a time, and when these are mastered, another set of 5 to 7 may be introduced. What does this say about assigning 20 new words each week or the practice of vocabulary workbooks? Those who want more in-depth vocabulary development strategies may want to obtain a copy of Janet Allen's *Words, Words, Words.* Appropriate vocabulary development is essential to developing fluency and to developing comprehension of text, which is the expectation of upper elementary, middle, and high school content teachers.

Fluency

The next reading element focus for elementary through high school is fluency. Fluency is the bridge between word recognition and comprehension. This is the most neglected element of reading at the upper elementary, middle, and high school levels and, when attended to, will improve reading comprehension of content texts. Anything we do fluently, we do with appropriate speed and accuracy. In reading, fluency means that students can read with appropriate rate, expression, and phrasing. Those students who stutter and struggle when decoding (calling out the words) cannot focus their mental energy on comprehension because all of their effort is focused on just getting the words out. These students need assistance in developing fluency in reading content texts so they can remember what they read.

How can content teachers assist with the element of fluency while teaching their standards-based content? Fluency comes with practice and after listening to proficient models. Before students are asked to read a text, they should first learn the essential new vocabulary. Then the teacher may want to point out passages in the text that have the greatest influence on comprehension of the key points. While pointing out these important passages, the teacher should read them aloud to the students as they follow along. Having heard key passages read by a fluent model, followed by discussion of the vocabulary in context and the meaning of the passages discussed, students will be poised for success in reading entire passages silently and independently.

Teachers must ensure that when passages from a textbook are read aloud to the entire class, the reader is fluent. Some examples of fluent readers include the teacher, an audiotape that accompanies the textbook, or a compact disk (CD or DVD) or Web sites that accompany and support the textbook. Within the class, there may be other fluent readers who can assist with reading aloud passages that are important to understanding the concepts and content of the chapter. Hearing fluent readers, as well as individually reading and rereading passages, improves fluency.

At this point, teachers often ask, "What about round robin reading?" Teachers often have the entire class read a chapter aloud, rotating the reading from student to student. The purpose given by the teachers for the round robin reading is to ensure that all students read the chapter. When asked the result, these teachers often respond that the poor readers still do not understand the text, and when the struggling readers read aloud they frustrate the better readers and the other struggling ones. The end result is that round robin reading advances neither fluency nor understanding of the content text, and it provides struggling readers with less than fluent models, hindering their reading comprehension improvement in content classrooms.

Language arts and reading teachers should teach fluency directly. Poetry, short passages, or interesting text may be read and reread over a period of time for practice in phrasing, intonation, and emphasis. Students may read and reread passages in pairs or triads until they read perfectly without hesitation. Taping readings, followed by listening and retaping, can also assist readers in hearing how they read and in improving. Choral reading can provide safety for students reading aloud while at the same time providing practice in repeated reading. Adding multimedia projects to literacy practice can assist with fluency when students are video- or audiotaped and the recording is added to a presentation.

Let me (Rose) share an example of reading and rereading that developed fluency and improved comprehension with older, struggling readers. A colleague, Rick McAtee, was asked to work with male prisoners in Canada who were reading at levels from first to fifth grade. Although the prison had historically had a reading program in which inmates with good behavior could enroll, the reading gains were not satisfactory. One of the issues was that to improve reading, students had to practice on their independent reading level to get better, and these inmates (adolescent and adult males) were not about to be seen with books on their reading level—children's books! McAtee provided the inmates with motivation by asking them to record readings of children's books, which would be given, along with the book, to local elementary schools for the use of each school's struggling readers. The inmates read and reread the same book as many as 50 times to get the recording just right for the children! As a result of this reading and rereading at the inmates' reading levels, their fluency and comprehension increased 2.6 years in 12 months, as measured by the Scholastic Reading Inventory (Taylor & McAtee, 2003). This same thing could have been done in any middle or high school classroom with struggling readers. Fluency, followed by comprehension, develops from reading and rereading.

Comprehension

Most teachers go straight to the expectation that students read and comprehend content text when beginning a new unit. Teachers may introduce new vocabulary, then assign the reading of text with the expectation that students will understand it. By instructing students in comprehension, rather than assigning reading, teachers can make sure that students will understand what they read, remember what they read, and be able to communicate to others what they have read. Instruction of comprehension of text can be provided through the teaching, modeling, and practicing of literacy strategies until students own them and can select the ones that best suit their purposes. Certain comprehension strategies appear to provide more gain in student achievement than others. Following are some to begin with and to expect consistent use of by teachers:

- monitoring of understanding
- using semantic and graphic organizers
- generating and answering questions
- recognizing text structure
- summarizing
- visualization
- prediction
- clarification
- connecting to self, other text, and the world

Deliberate and purposeful instruction on strategies to use before reading, during reading, and after reading enhances comprehension of content text while developing better readers and writers (Taylor, 2003).

The five elements of reading identified by NCLB are incorporated into the fail-safe literacy point of view discussed in the next section. This point of view is designed to make the challenge of creating joyful, independent readers, writers, and content learners a reasonable reality for every school, pre-kindergarten through twelfth grade.

THE FAIL-SAFE LITERACY POINT OF VIEW

How do these five elements of reading operationalize at all school levels? What is reasonable for teachers who are expected to be content experts and to teach a standards-based curriculum in their content area? To answer these questions, we will take a journey through the fail-safe literacy point of view, which is consistent with NCLB and grounded in the following (nonnegotiable) research-based literacy expectations for daily practice.

- Teachers use the processes of literacy: reading, writing, speaking, viewing, listening, thinking, and expressing through multiple symbol systems.
- Teachers read to and with students.
- Teachers teach, model, and practice the strategies of expert readers and writers.
- Students read independently, with accountability.

As you read the examples of the nonnegotiable expectations for daily practice, take note of how they are deliberately infused into teaching techniques before reading, during reading, and after reading. Many teachers use the nonnegotiables before reading, but few consistently frame instruction before, during, and after reading, although it is this practice that will best build vocabulary, fluency, and comprehension at a higher level.

Students can read independently when they know about 95% of the vocabulary in a text, which probably means reading on grade level and reading on grade-level text. On the other hand, with deliberate and purposeful incorporation of the daily nonnegotiables, including framing print instruction with literacy strategies before, during, and after reading, students can access text if they only know about 75% of the vocabulary. Teachers should determine the extent of support required, depending on the difficulty of the text for the students. The fail-safe literacy point of view provides access to content text that students cannot access otherwise.

Processes of Literacy

If you have children or have observed infants, think back to the first time you thought the infant could listen and think. Most people will remember an instance even prior to birth when the infant responded to a particular voice, such as the father's. Then, after birth, it is not long—sometimes in the birthing room—when the infant hears a familiar voice and turns and responds to that voice. As the days go by, infants view the world around them while their parents and caregivers talk to them about their family, community, colors, shapes, numbers, and other concepts we later teach in school. Before speaking, babies are listening, viewing, and thinking.

When babies utter those first words—Mom-ma, Da-da—we are so excited because not only do they speak, *they show that they know* who these people are. They show that *they associate language with meaning.* They have learned to speak through their experience in listening, viewing, and thinking. For the next several years, we work hard to teach our children many words and concepts through these literacy processes of listening, viewing, speaking, and thinking. We also introduce concepts of print by reading to them from left to right, holding the book, and noting the title. When our babies begin to speak in complete sentences, they often surprise us with the in-depth vocabulary and content concepts they have learned, as well as with their ability to communicate those concepts. Keep in mind that up to this point, they are not readers and have never been drilled with flash cards or assigned to read a chapter in a textbook!

Around the time they begin kindergarten or first grade, these children who have developed their oral language are introduced to print, with the expectation that they will make meaning of that print. Those with rich oral language backgrounds will be able to learn to read quite easily and then learn to write. Together, they are developing their reading and writing skills (Taylor, 2003). The fail-safe literacy point of view encourages teachers of pre-kindergarten through third grade to equalize the reading of nonfiction and fiction texts in the classroom to engage those who enjoy each type of literature (boys particularly) and to build content vocabulary and concepts. Not only will it improve student achievement in elementary schools, it will have a dramatic impact in later grades when almost the entire focus of school is on nonfiction and informational text. Certainly the focus of standardized assessment is skewed in that direction! We cannot expect students to perform well in reading assessments when their reading experience is unlike the reading assessment text.

Following this scenario of how language naturally develops through listening, viewing, thinking, and speaking prior to reading and writing, the fail-safe literacy point of view encourages all teachers to use all of the processes of literacy (reading, writing, speaking, listening, viewing, thinking, and expressing through multiple symbol systems) to introduce and teach all content concepts. Furthermore, as with the introduction of vocabulary, we believe that by using speaking, listening, viewing, multiple symbol systems, and thinking prior to reading and writing, students will more easily develop the language of the content so they can successfully build a scaffold that will help them access the printed text. The processes should also be used *during* reading to deepen understanding and *after* reading to demonstrate understanding and work at high levels of thinking.

Here is an example. When introducing *Romeo and Juliet,* the teacher introduces key vocabulary orally and relates it to language that the students know. Better yet, the students divide into groups and define the vocabulary in their own words. Then, perhaps, they see 5–10 minutes (not the entirety) of the movie *Romeo and Juliet,* to establish setting, voice, characters, and theme and to create a mental model of the play. After the vocabulary, content, and concepts are understood, reading of the text begins. This is the perfect unit in which to use the Internet for research, use DVDs, view video clips of scenes, role play, and access and create knowledge through multiple symbol systems for long-term learning.

Typically, teachers save field trips, lab experiences, hands-on experiences, and multimedia for rewards for learning rather than using them at the beginning of the unit, as suggested with *Romeo and Juliet.* Teachers who accept the concept of language development and how it relates to vocabulary, concept, and content learning will provide these rich experiences prior to the reading of text to build vocabulary and concept knowledge so that students will more easily have access to the comprehension of the printed text. Multiple symbol systems are an understood language of our students and assist in providing access to content learning and in the development of readers and writers. Teachers who try this approach find that it is successful with more students than is the traditional approach of assigning reading first and having viewing, listening, multiple symbol systems, and speaking experiences later in the unit.

Reading to and With Students

Why would reading to and with students be included in a book on creating a literacy system that includes students in and beyond elementary school? When I ask teachers this question, the first response is "They love for us to read to them!" and "Students understand when I read a passage but don't understand it when they read it independently." Following the line of thinking that oral language develops prior to written language, reading to students and with students provides students with access to standards-based curricula if they are not reading on grade level, and this is true for students all the way through Grade 12. We read to and with students using grade-level texts to provide equal access to content curriculum and literature that students cannot access by reading independently. In contrast, reading essential paragraphs or sentences to students and supporting this with discussion gives students access to on-grade-level, standards-based curricula. Reading entire chapters aloud is not suggested and can consume valuable learning time.

While reading aloud to students, teachers model the use of strategies of expert readers and support the students in practicing them. Before reading aloud, the teacher asks students to look at the text and predict what it may be about from titles, pictures, the author, or words in boldface type. In science, social studies, and mathematics, students should preview the text, including maps, charts, and graphs. After previewing the text, teachers should ask students to write one-sentence conclusions about the text.

During the reading, students will confirm or disprove predictions, make more predictions, and develop questions. A good practice is to ask students to log their questions as they read.

After reading, good teachers ask students to make connections to other things that have been read and to themselves. Ask students, "What do you still want to know about the content or concept, and where will you find the information?" Taking time for students to develop an interest that is personal and to pursue it generates deeper thought, knowledge, and understanding.

Reading aloud is not entertainment, although it is enjoyable and motivates students to read independently. After teachers read aloud to students, many students will independently read the same text, which they never would have attempted prior to the read-aloud experience. Reading to and with students improves fluency, vocabulary development, comprehension, and joy of reading. Reading to and with students may also incorporate technology, such as CDs and audiotapes. To learn more about reading to and with students in all content areas, you may want to read *Yellow Brick Roads,* by J. Allen.

Teaching, Modeling, and Practicing the Strategies of Expert Readers and Writers

So far, two nonnegotiable expectations for daily practice have been discussed: using the processes of literacy and reading to and with students. The third nonnegotiable expectation for daily practice is to teach, model, and practice the strategies of expert readers. Frequently I find that schools have professional development sessions on many strategies, as well as graphic organizers, so teachers are aware that using strategies is a good thing to do in all classes. Notice that the nonnegotiable expectation is not *using* strategies but *teaching, modeling,* and *practicing* the strategies of expert readers. Keep in mind that the extent to which literacy strategies are employed depends on the level of difficulty of the text for the students. Employment of literacy strategies should take place before reading, during reading, and after reading.

Let me (Rose) share why this distinction is so important. When I was a middle school principal in a diverse school with high poverty, about 40% of the students were reading below grade level. At the time, there was a reading resource teacher, Nancy, whom I believed then and believe now is the best middle level reading resource teacher I have ever seen. She had worked with the teachers tirelessly on using strategies, and I observed their regular use as I walked through classrooms. Although it was against the trends of the time, I documented growth in students in reading from year to year and knew the students were making progress but not enough to close the gap. As Nancy and I grappled with the need to enhance growth in reading of more than a year for each year in school, we came to this conclusion: The *teachers* knew and used strategies, but the *students* did not know and use strategies. *Therefore, it is imperative to teach, model, and practice the strategies of expert readers and writers so that students develop ownership and will know which ones to use for comprehension when reading independently.*

When the LLT is developing a fail-safe literacy system, it will want to consider a systematic approach for all students receiving instruction in strategies, and it must create an expectation that all teachers teach, model, and practice strategies. At Southwest Middle School in Orlando, Florida, each team of teachers developed a plan for how they would teach, model, and practice the strategies of expert readers. Their principal and resource teacher supported them in this critical effort to improve literacy and content learning for their students. The place to begin is with the literacy strategies that seem to make the most difference in comprehension and achievement gains, as mentioned in the section on NCLB. Consider these:

- prediction
- clarification
- visualization

- question asking and question answering
- summarization
- recognizing text structure
- evaluation
- making connections to self, other text, and the world

Of the strategies listed, prediction and summarization are probably the most commonly employed. Students who are not good readers do not visualize when their eyes pass over print, so teaching and using visualization as a strategy is key to reaching all learners. Visualization is not just what we see; it includes all of our senses—smell, touch, taste, and hearing.

Each school is encouraged to consider carefully teaching question and answer relationships, such as those found in *Teaching Reading in the Content Area: If Not Me, Then Who?* (Billmeyer & Barton, 1998). When all teachers are expected to teach and use the four levels of questions and all students are expected to generate and answer the four levels of questions, learning can only go up. If students understand the kinds of questions and can find the answers, then they can provide the answers when requested. This strategy is probably the one that is least used, but it is the one that can have the greatest impact on measurable student achievement.

For more information on the strategies of expert readers and how to teach students these strategies, you will find *Teaching Reading in the Content Area: If Not Me, Then Who?* (Billmeyer & Barton, 1998); *Reader's Handbook* (Robb, 2002); and *Strategies That Work* (Harvey & Goudvis, 2000) to be excellent resources.

Read Independently With Accountability

So far, the nonnegotiable expectations of daily practice have reflected reordering the use of the processes of literacy; reading to and with students; and teaching, modeling, and practicing the strategies of expert readers. These nonnegotiables are all teacher instructional behaviors, meant to develop students' vocabulary, fluency, and comprehension, so that they can access content curriculum independently through reading and writing. Accountable independent reading is the time when students practice what they have learned through implementation of the first three nonnegotiables.

Think about people you know who are really expert at something—maybe golf, playing a musical instrument, singing, negotiating, public speaking, or anything else. How often do these experts practice? Chances are you are thinking, "Every day, often more than once." Anything we do well, we practice over and over again to get better at it. The same thing goes for reading. If we want students to read at a higher level, then they must practice at their independent reading level and keep increasing that level to get better.

Those students who are excellent readers, who read in the 90th percentile, probably read independently at least 30 minutes each day; those in the 70th percentile probably read independently about 20 minutes each day. With these time frames in mind, it is recommended that students read independently, with accountability, at least 20 minutes each day to practice the strategies of expert readers that they have been taught and to build fluency, vocabulary, and comprehension. As mentioned, when students are in accountable independent reading, they are reading, on their independent reading level, something they find interesting and have chosen. If they are to accomplish this, their teacher must have a classroom library that spans the independent reading levels and interest levels of the students. Teachers may secure large selections from the school library and rotate selections throughout the year as their curriculum changes. Books should be respectful of the students' developmental stage, culture, and background. Having at least 50% of the books be nonfiction is important for building content vocabulary, concepts, and knowledge and for engaging students at all grade levels who enjoy nonfiction. The percentage of nonfiction reading should mirror the percentage of nonfiction reading expected on standardized assessments. For instance, if the percentage is 70, then students should be reading 70% nonfiction. Teachers must also know the reading levels of the students and the books if they are to coach students in their book selection. Choice is a critical motivator for accountable independent reading.

In contrast to free reading, or "drop everything and read" time, students are not just reading anything; they are reading books for which the teacher will hold them accountable. This accountability does not mean a test but some literacy-related accountability, such as a reading log, a log of daily connections the student makes to the reading, a book talk to the class, a book advertisement, artwork, or some form of accountability agreed on by the teacher and the student. Choice in how the student demonstrates accountability is important for motivating those readers who struggle. Most struggling students shy away from tests, since they have experienced lack of success with them. The students that need the greatest engagement with accountable independent reading are those reading below the 50th percentile.

Accountability has another implication. With the expectation of ongoing monitoring of reading achievement, neither teachers nor principals can afford to wait until the annual formal assessment to see if students are improving. The teacher who is responsible for accountable independent reading should have periodic classroom assessments, such as the *Degrees of Reading Power*, published by Touchtone Applied Science Associates, Inc., or the *Scholastic Reading Inventory* (SRI), published by Scholastic, Inc., which provide reading comprehension growth information and can assist in directing students to reading that is appropriate for their reading level, age, and interests. At any time, the principal should be able to access student and classroom data on progress made in reading during the school year.

While every teacher assigns independent reading of content text and works with students on their vocabulary, fluency, and comprehension of those texts, the LLT will need to carefully consider which teachers will be responsible for accountable independent reading. There are many scheduling options to consider, and each school will be different. In Grades 1–6, this may be the expectation for all students, so the reading or language arts teacher will have the responsibility. To accomplish accountable independent reading in middle school, students might have language arts every day for a double period, mathematics every day for a double period, and science and social studies on alternate days.

Another option might be that only students reading below the 50th percentile be required to have accountable independent reading in Grades 6–12. These students would be scheduled into a double language arts period every day. The second part of the language arts period would replace one of the students' electives. The remainder of the schedule would be the same for all students. The main point is that students who read below grade level need more time to practice to improve their reading levels.

In a discussion with principals on the issue of how to accomplish these expectations, it became clear that the scheduling of accountable independent reading was the most challenging because it has time, space, personnel, and budget implications. In the summer of 2002, Tim Cool, principal of Stone Middle School, came up to me and said, "Rose, I just can't do this. My elective teachers and coaches will kill me! The students will rebel; they are the ones who need elective outlets the most." My response to him was, "I know you live in a political environment. Only you can determine your level of commitment to students reading on grade level when they leave your middle school. Do you want them to be expert basketball players or expert readers?" Maybe this response seems harsh, but we must be honest about our level of commitment and have it reflected in our words, actions, and budget. At the end of the day, Cool came to me and thanked me for being frank and said that he thought he had figured out a way to make it work. A few months later, he sent more of his LLT to visit with me regarding implementation. At the end of one year, his school's grade, based on improvements in reading for students in each quartile, rose from a C to an A! Cool is committed to literacy learning and to continued improvement in each student score quartile.

Nonnegotiable Expectations of Daily Practice

We have just reviewed the nonnegotiables of daily practice that are the foundation of the fail-safe literacy point of view and that support NCLB. When I (Rose) introduce these four nonnegotiables, teachers often nod and acknowledge that some of them do some of these things sometimes. The critical difference in improving reading, writing, and content learning is that teachers are expected to do these things every day, consistently. This consistency will yield measurable gains in student achievement. Ideally, teachers will develop instructional plans clearly identifying what they will do before reading, during reading, and after reading to provide access to standards-based, on-grade-level text for those who read below grade level. All teachers would be expected to use the processes of literacy; read to and with students; and teach, model, and practice the strategies of expert readers to provide students with equal access to a standards-based content curriculum. The LLT will plan for accountable independent reading in a way that supports all students becoming joyful, independent readers, writers, and content learners.

FAIL-SAFE LITERACY LEADERS COLLABORATING ACROSS CONTENT AREAS

Two different real school approaches to collaboration for developing a literacy system follow, offering you ideas for broad-scale collaboration. One approach occurred in a high school, one in a large district.

Sebastian River High School

Sebastian River is a high school of about 1300 students, serving a largely blue collar community (with about 40% of the students on free or reduced-fee lunch) in Indian River County, Florida. The administration, faculty, and staff are focused on each student reaching his or her potential. Upon arriving on campus as a visitor, I (Rose) was immediately impressed with the feeling of calm and the welcome that

I felt from both students and faculty. This culture of cohesiveness and family is what many high schools unsuccessfully strive to achieve. Even with this positive school culture, however, the faculty was not satisfied with student achievement.

The administration created an LLT representing all departments and grade levels. A full day workshop was set up, with follow-up sessions for the LLT and any other faculty members who wanted to attend. Following the establishment of a research base and teacher use of the nonnegotiables, the LLT participated in a day-long planning session. After the LLT drafted out the literacy system, it was revised with input from faculty, and implementation began.

Follow-up evaluation for Year 2 of the implementation and commensurate revision of the system was taking place as this was written. Review of data on current students and incoming ninth grade students (50% read on Level 1 or 2) were driving revisions that included intervention for Level 1 readers (lowest) and intervention for Level 2 readers (second lowest). In-class coaching visits and after-school professional development were scheduled for all faculty and learning communities. At Sebastian River High School, the principal and all assistant principals participate fully in each professional development experience, demonstrating their sincere commitment to their teachers.

Lake County Public Schools

Superintendent Pam Saylor recognized that her district's students were not performing as well as they could and that literacy held the key. By establishing that literacy was the number one priority for the diverse, 30,000-student district, the elementary and secondary supervisors took action to develop a comprehensive district literacy system with broad-scale input: *Just Read, Lake!*

The first step was for me (Rose) to meet with the district elementary and secondary supervisors to develop a timeline and action plan that began in February 2003 and extended through 2004. We knew that the system would involve large numbers, so a timeline had to be adhered to for needed changes to be considered in next year's district budget and for schools to plan for modifying their budgets, as well as personnel selection, professional development, and schedules.

Four facilitated sessions took place, creating common language and understanding of research on literacy learning. Following the establishment of and agreement on the research base, participants worked on the components of the literacy system that you will find in Chapters 3–5 of this book. Participants were elementary, middle, and high school administrators, teachers, literacy coaches, library and media specialists, and district personnel.

These drafts were synthesized to honor the needs and requests of those who participated. The draft system was edited and reviewed by a core team at the district level. Next, all participants were invited to a session to walk through the system, to understand, respond, question, and gain commitment and support for the final document. Excellent input regarding perceived meaning and implications of particular sections was given, resulting in a refined *Just Read, Lake!*

Two large issues arose during the development of *Just Read, Lake!* The first was the need for an electronic system that would manage student data and work with various assessments. A district team worked together to develop a system of assessments and management of the data so that teachers and administrators would easily be able to monitor ongoing development of reading.

The second issue was providing consistent professional development at the schools for all faculty and staff. This concern resulted in the budgeting of a literacy coach for each school, accompanied by collaborative development of nine Essential Core Professional Development Modules for *Just Read, Lake!* These modules are discussed in detail in Chapter 5.

Superintendent Saylor presented the system to the school board. Each principal received the PowerPoint presentation and script so that a consistent overview would be shared with every faculty and staff member during the days before school opening in August 2003.

REVIEW AND REFLECTION

When I (Rose) think back over the last several years of working with schools and districts in developing literacy systems, several themes always emerge.

- First, those that make gains develop a practitioner-friendly system with genuine intent to implement. This system is not one for a notebook on a shelf but one that will have coffee stains and wear out with use!
- The literacy system development is preceded by the establishment of a research base and common language.
- Administrators and leadership must be willing to hear and incorporate input from everyone, even input that does not feel good.

- Broad-scale participation is invited, respected, and reflected in the system. No one's input is rejected or put down.
- Commitment is established to provide for the needs identified: personnel, materials, technology, professional development, structure, assessment, data management.

Schools who enter into the fail-safe literacy system planning process with the intent of creating trust and consistency in literacy learning behaviors on a daily basis meet with success that can be measured and celebrated as students become better readers, writers, and content learners.

HELPFUL TERMS

Comprehension: Understanding what is read so that it can be communicated.

Fluency: Reading with appropriate rate, expression, and phrasing.

Intensive reading: Intervention classes or action for those reading two or more years below grade level.

Intervention: Classes or action taken specifically for those students reading two or more years below grade level.

Literacy leadership team (LLT): A collaborative team representing all stakeholders who work together to infuse scientific, research-based practices of literacy throughout the school.

Nonnegotiables of daily practice: Instructional expectations of all teachers that must be infused into their practice all day long.

Phonics: The relationship between letters and written language and their sounds.

Phonemic awareness: The ability to hear, identify, and manipulate the individual sounds in spoken words.

Processes of literacy: Reading, writing, speaking, listening, viewing, thinking, and expressing through multiple symbol systems.

Vocabulary: The words we must know if we are to communicate when listening, speaking, reading, and writing.

FURTHER READING AND RESOURCES

Allen, J. (1999). *Words, words, words: Teaching vocabulary in Grades 4–12.* Portland, ME: Stenhouse.

Allen, J. (2000). *Yellow brick roads: Shared and guided paths to independent reading 4–12*. Portland, ME: Stenhouse.

Barton, M. L., & Heidman, C. (2002). *Teaching reading in mathematics* (2nd ed.). Aurora, CO: McREL.

Barton, M. L., & Jordan, D. L. (2001). *Teaching reading in science*. Aurora, CO: McREL.

Biancarosa, G., & Snow, C. E. (2004, October). *Reading next: A vision for action and research in middle and high school literacy* (Report). New York: Carnegie Corporation.

Billmeyer, R., & Barton, M. L. (1998). *Teaching reading in the content areas: If not me, then who?* Aurora, CO: McREL.

Burns, M. S., & Griffen, P. (1999). *Starting out right: A guide to promoting children's reading success*. Washington, DC: National Academy Press.

Collins, J. (2001). *Good to great*. New York: Harper Business.

Educational Research Service. (2002). *Helping struggling readers at the elementary and secondary levels*. Arlington, VA: Author.

Rasinki, T. V. (2003). *The fluent reader: Oral reading strategies for building word recognition, fluency, and comprehension*. New York: Scholastic.

Robb, L. (2002). *Reader's handbook*. Wilmington, MA: Great Source.

Snow, C., Burns, M. S., & Griffin, P. (Eds.). (1998). *Preventing reading difficulties in young children*. Washington, DC: National Academy Press.

Taylor, R. T., & McAtee, R. (2003, March). Turning a new page to life and literacy. *Journal of Adolescent and Adult Literacy, 46*(6), 478–480.

Wilson, E. A. (2004). *Reading at the middle and high school levels* (3rd ed.). Arlington, VA: Educational Research Service.

Description of the process to develop *Just Read, Lake!* and the resulting plan is used with permission of Lake County Schools, Florida.

3 Developing the Literacy System Through Collaboration

STEP 1: COMMITTING TO FAIL-SAFE LITERACY LEADERSHIP

- Reflect on your literacy leadership.
- Focus on the result of all students becoming joyful, independent readers, writers, and content learners.
- Review the scientifically based research on literacy.
- Establish a plan and timeline for development.
- Create your representative literacy leadership team.

As a literacy leader, you have reflected on your leadership and perhaps even gathered feedback from faculty on the APEL to see how they perceive implementation of the four constructs in your school. You may have taken steps to strengthen evidence of these constructs. Next you established an LLT representing all stakeholders within the school community. Then you got down to work to be sure that the LLT and faculty had a good understanding of the research on literacy learning and the expectations of NCLB. Now you are ready to get started on developing a fail-safe literacy system for your school.

The underpinnings of the process that follows are as follows:

- the culture of trust is established
- genuine input and discussion is desired and facilitated

At this point, you should establish a plan and time frame, with checkpoints for facilitating input, sharing the draft with others, editing, and finalizing the system for implementation. Each of these checkpoints is key to having a literacy system with maximized implementation. Making a calendar that includes target dates, meeting purposes, editing time frames, the rollout date, and all events in the process is very important. An example was provided in Chapter 2 with *Just Read, Lake!* Planning for the people who will be involved; when the involvement takes place; editing procedures; sharing with the involved stakeholders before others; and the official announcement, rollout, and presentation to school board members or the superintendent should be done with care.

One of your important decisions will be made when you answer the question, *"Who will facilitate the LLT or faculty in generating authentic input?"* Many of you will want to do it yourself or delegate it to your right-hand person. Keep in mind that the facilitator should be very comfortable with disagreement and negative input as well as with positive input. You will want to select a person who has enough knowledge of the school system and school (and literacy!) that he or she will ask for clarifications when needed to facilitate a useful, content-rich system that will indeed make a measurable difference. Frequently, when I have facilitated literacy system input, participants have approached me afterward and marveled at how I handled disagreement or how I probed someone who was being general rather than specific. Whoever you select to facilitate should be confident and comfortable with every participant and not appear to be just going through the motions. With this and other decisions made, let's get started.

STEP 2: AGREEING ON A COMMON LANGUAGE TO DRIVE INSTRUCTION

After study to develop a common research base on literacy, the LLT is ready to begin with the charge they have been given: to create a doable, fail-safe literacy system for improving the reading, writing, and content learning of all the students in the school. With the research base understood, the first step in creating a literacy plan is to agree on a common language to be used within the school with teachers, parents, and students. This time for clarification of language is important, because words mean different things to different people.

When I begin the process of developing a literacy system, I (Rose) ask those at each table to take five minutes and define literacy, then post the definition on chart paper. At the end of five minutes, if there are five or even ten groups, each will define literacy a little differently. Through facilitation, we clarify what each group means in regard to each of the terms used and come to agreement on the definitions of these terms. This process serves to review and build the research knowledge and to make sure that we know what we are suggesting. Here are some definitions groups recently wrote and shared.

Literacy:

"Read, write, and speak in your home language."

"Read orally, comprehend, write"

"Read, apply, synthesize"

"Read, digest, and regurgitate what you learned" (from the physical educators)

"Decoding, vocabulary, fluency, and comprehension" (from the reading teachers)

"Literacy is reading, writing, and communicating what you have read."

As each group shares, I take the opportunity to distinguish between reading orally, or "word calling," and reading to comprehend text, which is what the upper elementary, middle, and high school teachers expect. We usually agree that we need to clarify for students, parents, and all faculty that reading means comprehending, not just reading orally. Many students think reading means that their eyes pass over the print, but there is no expectation of processing the print. They might also think it means to decode orally, since most have experienced great emphasis on oral decoding in the elementary schools. Their prior experience of reinforcement for reading out loud may be the reason they all want to read out loud, even when they are not fluent. Clarifying expectations with students may not seem necessary, but it does help to make our teaching transparent for them.

In reviewing the examples that teacher groups generated, you will notice that there is only one complete sentence. When I make this observation (and I generally have no more than one complete sentence in a faculty of even 150 teachers), I like to have the teachers reflect on communication in its broader forms, which includes the arts, music, graphics, and many symbolic representations. There will usually be some teachers who illustrate their definitions or make graphic organizers, but always there will be divergent ways of representing their thinking.

After reflecting on their definitions and clarifying the meaning of what the groups wrote, we look for commonalities and draft a definition that they can accept. The key is that those defining literacy understand what it means and how it will be used in the context of their school or system. I encourage faculties to write research-based definitions to drive instruction, not to be placed in a notebook on a shelf. When the purpose of the common definition is perceived as having to drive instruction, a faculty or LLT will write the definition differently than if it is written to make the school look good or to serve a political purpose. An example that drives instruction is "Literacy is reading, writing, listening, and speaking." If that is the school's definition, it is defensible by faculty, as it represents standards commonly found across content areas. Also, teachers can be expected to include reading, writing, listening, and speaking in all instructional plans, regardless of content area. In its understanding of the concept of language development, the LLT may go so far as to recommend that teachers introduce vocabulary, concepts, and content orally first (listening and speaking), using concrete images that will create mental models. Then, after students have some understanding of the vocabulary and concepts to be learned, they can use it as a scaffold to reading and writing. In sum, the definition creates a common language that is research-based and drives instruction across the school. The LLT and faculty know the deeper meaning behind the definition and can explain, implement, and (if need be) defend it. Most important is that more students will have access to the standards-based curriculum.

The fail-safe point of view defines literacy as reading, writing, speaking, viewing, listening, thinking, and expressing through multiple symbol systems. This definition was explained in depth in the fail-safe point of view section of Chapter 2. Briefly, the fail-safe definition was written to drive instruction, with the expectation that all teachers will incorporate these processes of literacy as they design their instructional plans. Additionally, new content, concepts, and vocabulary would be introduced with viewing, listening, and thinking to build oral language, then speaking, followed by reading and writing after facility with the new information is achieved and the mental model is in place with the students.

STEP 3: AGREEING ON NONNEGOTIABLE EXPECTATIONS OF DAILY PRACTICE

Defining literacy is not so hard for a large group. Determining this definition is actually fun, and it energizes the group with all they know and learn in the collaborative process. Step 3, *agree on nonnegotiable expectations of daily practice,* is a little harder. I would suggest five or fewer nonnegotiables of daily practice. Generally, I recommend that if any group wants to be able to remember something or wants others to remember it, keep that "it" to a handful or less—that is, five or fewer. More than five may be supported in the research but is not practical for full-scale implementation across an entire faculty. Take a few minutes to discuss with the LLT what the implication is of identifying items as nonnegotiable expectations of daily practice. *Nonnegotiable* means it will happen every day, not when we have time, not after we finish the standards-based curriculum, not just on Fridays. Nonnegotiable expectations of daily practice infuse literacy into the teaching of standards-based curricula. Therefore daily consistency is the key to measurable improvement in reading, writing, and content learning. Careful consideration should be made in developing these nonnegotiables, as they are the basis for the support tools that are created in Chapter 7 to ensure implementation and measurement of success.

Asking the LLT or faculty to agree on expectations for everyone's classroom can be a challenge. The first thing they will do is reflect back on the research. What are the classroom practices that seem to consistently emerge in the literature on literacy, regardless of content area? Probable answers will be something like independent reading, reading strategies, graphic organizers, connecting reading and writing, and popular motivational programs. Some LLTs may mention that research encourages consistent practice or that those who read in the lower quartiles need more time for literacy development. You may wish to divide the LLT into 4 or 5 groups and ask each group to list 5 expectations for daily practice that are reasonable for all faculty members. Then share the lists and see which items are most prevalent and which ones the LLT can support for expectations of daily practice for all faculty. Although many excellent practices are likely to emerge, there will not be too many that LLT members are comfortable offering up as a daily expectation for all of their colleagues, regardless of content assignments!

The fail-safe literacy point of view discussed in Chapter 2 identified four nonnegotiable expectations of daily practice.

1. Teachers use the processes of literacy: reading, writing, speaking, viewing, listening, thinking, and expressing through multiple symbol systems.
2. Teachers read to and with students.
3. Teachers teach, model, and practice the strategies of expert readers.
4. Students read independently with accountability.

As described in the fail-safe point of view in Chapter 2, all teachers are expected to use the first three nonnegotiable expectations of daily practice to teach vocabulary, fluency, and comprehension of the standards-based curriculum content text. The fourth nonnegotiable expectation of daily practice takes some scheduling on the part of teachers and administrators, but this is where students practice independently what they have learned during the first three non-negotiables and improve in reading level.

In pre-kindergarten through eighth grade, all students should have accountable independent reading every day. In Grades 9–12, at least those students reading below grade level should have accountable independent reading.

Another potential nonnegotiable expectation of daily practice for consideration that will positively influence learning and is very doable is a literacy enriched, print-rich classroom. Whenever I (Rose) work with an entire faculty, LLT, or teachers from various schools, I always pause and ask them to raise their hands if they can commit to each of these daily nonnegotiables. Without fail, once the teachers understand them, they agree to make a real effort to include the nonnegotiables every day, regardless of their curriculum content or the grade level taught.

LITERACY LEADERSHIP TEAMS IN ACTION

This process sounds good, but how does it work with real faculty in schools and districts with immediate needs? An example follows that brings to light how agreement may develop on a common language and on the nonnegotiable expectations of daily practice. Examples from the finalized fail-safe literacy system are included.

Just Read, Lake!

Lake County Schools responded to their number one priority learning need of improving reading with the development of *Just*

Read, Lake! This program, with applications for pre-kindergarten through twelfth grade, is far reaching enough to address all grade levels and specific enough to be implemented and measured. Through the consistency created with the system, evaluation of its success and ensuing revisions can be made on a timely basis. *Just Read, Lake!* is the vehicle with which the district will meet its goal for all students to score Level 3 (on grade level) or higher on the Florida Comprehensive Assessment Test in reading, as well as meeting the annual yearly progress requirements. The collaborative process described in Chapter 2 involved more than 100 employees, representing diverse positions across the district and ensuring broad-scale involvement of stakeholders.

The five-year framework was developed to provide all students with the opportunity to be successful in school and in their adult lives. The driving force in the plan is to ensure the success of all students. *Literacy is defined as listening, viewing, thinking, speaking, reading, writing, and expressing through multiple symbol systems at a developmentally appropriate level* (*Just Read, Lake!*, p. 3). The definition includes the prepositional phrase "at a developmentally appropriate level" because of the age ranges addressed, which may be anywhere from 3–4 year olds to 18–19 year olds, in some cases. Reading appropriately at the second grade level is quite different than at the fifth or tenth grade level.

Unique to this definition is "expressing through multiple symbol systems," which refers to mathematics, maps, graphs, charts, symbols, music, art, movement, technology, and any communication system other than alphabetic print. Acknowledgment of the valuing of expressing through multiple symbol systems assists in the recruitment of teachers of all content courses. Furthermore, it validates incorporation of multiple ways of learning (through different strengths, such as tactile, kinesthetic, visual, verbal, mathematical, spatial), by which teachers can access prior knowledge and introduce new learning and students can show what they know, including comprehension of text.

Through the collaborative process, the district agreed on non-negotiable expectations for daily practice. Implementation district-wide, pre-kindergarten through twelfth grade, ensures student access to the standards-based curriculum in all subjects and improves reading achievement (*Just Read, Lake*!, p. 3).

- Instructors use the seven processes of literacy: listening, viewing, thinking, speaking, reading, writing and expressing through multiple symbol systems.
- Instructors teach, model, and practice strategies of expert readers and writers.

- Instructors read to and with students.
- Students read independently with accountability.
- Teachers of pre-K through Grade 1 levels incorporate phonemic awareness instruction.

These nonnegotiable expectations of daily practice are similar to those in the fail-safe point of view. Any that are research-based will appear similar and have unique components specific to the district or school environment. In this case, the second nonnegotiable, "Instructors teach, model, and practice strategies of expert readers and writers," acknowledges the relationship between developing reading and writing simultaneously and the importance at all grade levels of teaching, modeling, and practicing rather than assigning reading and writing.

You will also notice the last bullet, "Teachers of pre-K through Grade 1 levels incorporate phonemic awareness instruction." This is an essential daily expectation for the primary grades and, stated here, leaves no doubt that phonemic awareness instruction will be monitored. Discussion took place during the writing and editing about creating an explicit nonnegotiable related to phonemic awareness for other grades, but the decision was made to have only five nonnegotiable expectations of daily practice. Having only five means that there are only five that must take place, but this does not eliminate the appropriate assumption on the part of teachers or administrators that other research-based practices would take place. For instance, if there are students in grades beyond Grade 1 who need phonemic awareness instruction, then most assuredly teachers are responsible for attending to the need.

REVIEW AND REFLECTION

The success of any literacy system will depend on how doable it is by all stakeholders. For it to be fail-safe, it must be research-based but communicated in such a way that everyone can access it, just as we want all students to access standards-based curricula. In the past, I (Rose) have observed many school improvement plans, often written in esoteric language—certainly not written in meaningful ways that translated to classroom practice, except with the superstar teachers. To improve reading, writing, and content learning for *all students* hinges on *all teachers* having substantive roles to play and being able to play those roles successfully. The fail-safe literacy system is intended to engage all teachers and all learners all day long. Being accessible by all teachers does not reduce the rigor, because just as with students, the skillful leader will provide support, coaching, and guidance to access the rigorous expectations. Fail-safe literacy systems have these characteristics, some of which we will address in the following chapters:

- They are research-based.
- They address literacy, not just reading.
- The term *literacy* is defined.
- A common language is used that is accessible to all.
- There are five or fewer nonnegotiable expectations for daily practice.
- Details of the literacy system emerge from the nonnegotiables of daily practice.
- They have top administrative support and commensurate funding.
- Authentic input from stakeholders is encouraged.
- They are developmental in approach, creating a community of learners across the school or district.
- Required components of NCLB and adequate yearly progress have been addressed.
- They create an aligned system of literacy.
- They are future oriented, not past oriented.

HELPFUL TERMS

Common language: Vocabulary essential to creating a research-based plan is discussed and the meaning attributed to that vocabulary agreed on and written into the literacy plan.

Facilitator: An objective professional with content knowledge of literacy and ease in communication with all levels of faculty and staff who guides the process of collaboration in developing the literacy plan in the context of research and the unique school or district setting.

Multiple symbol systems: Symbol systems other than alphabetic, such as music, art, movement, mathematics, graphics, graphs, technology, charts, maps, and so on.

Nonnegotiable expectations of daily practice: Five or fewer literacy infusion expectations that all faculty will agree to implement. These expectations provide the consistency needed to improve reading, writing, and content learning and to measure that improvement.

FURTHER READING AND RESOURCES

Just read, lake! (2003). Taveres, FL: Lake County Schools. Lake County School System Web site: http://www.lake.k12.fl.us/. Readers may also e-mail the contact person for the district, Dr. Dale Moxley, at moxleyd@lake.k12.fl.us.

National Reading Panel. (2000). *Teaching children to read: An evidence-based assessment of the scientific research literature on reading and its implications for reading instruction.* Washington, DC: U.S. Department of Health and Human Services.

Robb, L. (2002). *Reader's handbook: Content area guide.* Wilmington, MA: Great Source.

Snow, C., Burns, M. S., & Griffin, P. (Eds.). (1998). *Preventing reading difficulties in young children.* Washington, DC: National Academy Press.

4 Using Exemplars to Kick Up Literacy Learning a Notch

Creating a consistent research-based expectation for every teacher to incorporate into practice all day long is the beginning of providing all students with access to a standards-based curriculum and of creating readers, writers, and content learners. Steps 1, 2, and 3 created the basis for upward spiraling of learning with the development of a common language and agreement on nonnegotiable expectations of daily practice. In addition to using nonnegotiable expectations of daily practice as a basis, the fail-safe literacy leader will collaborate with the LLT or entire faculty to create exemplars for which to strive and specific roles and responsibilities related to literacy learning.

Have you ever watched Emeril Lagasse, the famous New Orleans chef, on television? When he wants to make his dishes special (as he does on every television show), what does he do? He tosses in extra spices or perhaps a little vodka and—"Kabamm!"—*kicks it up a notch,* with lots of passion and enthusiasm added in! Next, Emeril finishes his dishes and serves them to the audience amid oohs and ahhs. Now, that is accountability! Step 4 *kicks learning up a notch* by clearly identifying exemplars and nonexemplars for every teacher across all content areas; use these exemplars, and you will see enthusiasm develop.

Step 5, clarifying roles and responsibilities, provides clear accountability for every stakeholder, related to literacy learning on the spot, in front of everyone.

Since Steps 4 and 5 kick learning up a notch and provide expectations for accountability, they also establish professional development goals for many stakeholders to work toward. For these steps particularly, you may want to consider involvement of the entire faculty rather than just the LLT.

STEP 4: CREATING EXEMPLARS AND NONEXEMPLARS

Automatically, the LLT or entire faculty will want to create exemplars for the reading teacher or the intervention teacher, but how about the mathematics teacher, the vocational teacher, and the art teacher? Did the LLT include these teachers in the nonnegotiables? How about the media specialist or librarian? What is exemplary and what is nonexemplary in regard to literacy infusion in each content area? Asking these questions will put a little positive pressure on everyone, because now literacy learning is getting specific, up close, and personal.

This is the beginning of real change. Now, you may be thinking that this is not just a literacy system planning process but professional development also. You are correct. The LLT or entire faculty is not writing an action plan for someone else. They are using research to identify teacher behaviors that will affect student achievement in a measurable way in their classrooms. They are committing to exemplars that they will learn about and implement, replacing perhaps some less exemplary practices that are comfortable but that do not yield acceptable gains in student achievement. These nonexemplary practices may have yielded gains in the past, but are now typical, so the learning curve has flattened, inviting new exemplars to be put into place. As one teacher recently emphatically stated to me: "Rose, I know to do all of these things. I just have to decide to do them." This is exactly where a number of teachers find themselves. They are aware of research-based practices that are exemplary, and they can articulate them. However, they have not committed to replacing typical, good teaching with exemplary teaching that will kick learning up a notch. This commitment, not knowledge, is what you are seeking.

Exemplars create mental models of excellence, compared to nonexemplars, which represent typical practice, or the status quo. Nonexemplars are not opposite to exemplars; they are not bad practice. Nonexemplars represent what teachers may be doing, so continuing the practice will maintain achievement, but not improve it. The old adage "If you keep doing what you are doing, you'll keep getting what you've gotten" is true in the case of teaching and learning also. Experiencing the development of exemplars and nonexemplars makes the fail-safe literacy system meaningful for all teachers across content areas. The LLT will proceed from the research-based non-negotiable expectations of daily practice to the development of five or six specific exemplary expectations for each content area: English or language arts, mathematics, science, social studies, second language learning, and electives. I would also encourage the creation of exemplars for library and media specialists, because their role is critical to the improvement of reading, writing, and content learning. Some believe that implementing exemplary practices in the library and media center can improve reading achievement by as much as 6%!

Facilitating the Exemplar Strategy

When introducing the concept of exemplars and nonexemplars, I first offer the terms to the group and ask them to tell me what *exemplar* means. Then, as a group, we clarify. Carefully, I explain that nonexemplars are not bad. In fact, they are probably good practice and probably found throughout the school. This clarification makes it safe for teachers to own their daily practice and to openly identify it. Because these practices are common, they will not increase student achievement. To increase student achievement, the typical practice must be enhanced to be exemplary; hence the creation of exemplars.

Teachers will volunteer that they do some or all of the exemplars that are identified. These teachers are role models and can be resources for creating consistent implementation across each content area. Generally, they will also add that they do the exemplars sometimes, but not consistently. *Consistent exemplary practice is what will improve student achievement.*

Why create both exemplars and nonexemplars? If the LLT or faculty only create exemplars, they will have targets to shoot for but will not have identified teaching behaviors to be replaced. Teachers are overwhelmed with all of the pressures placed on them, and they need permission to let go of some practices and replace them with other, more productive practices. Psychologically, as well as in reality, we are asking teachers to do a handful of things *differently*, not to do *more*. For many teachers, this is a relief.

After a brief discussion with the group related to what exemplars and nonexemplars are, model for them a couple of exemplars, just as we expect teachers to do with students when introducing a new concept. For example, let's consider reading, since that is the topic at hand. Look at Figure 4.1, Exemplar Example. There are three exemplars and nonexemplars listed to clarify between practice that should advance learning and practice that may be common and probably will not advance learning. Think about two or three more exemplars and nonexemplars and add them to Figure 4.1. The facilitator will do the same with the group. Provide an example, then ask the group to create a few more, and add them to the list so everyone sees how easy it is. Be sure to emphasize that these are research-based practices, not cute or creative ideas only. You might ask the group to identify one exemplar and nonexemplar related to fluency, then one of each for vocabulary, and then for comprehension, since those are the reading elements generally addressed. If you are working with teachers of prekindergarten through twelfth grades, you may want to add phonemic awareness and phonics.

Notice that this example only has six places for exemplars and nonexemplars. Remember, if we want teachers to change their behavior, we should only identify five or so items to be exemplars—just a

Figure 4.1 Exemplar Example

Content Area: Reading Intervention	
Note: Nonnegotiable expectations for daily practice are assumed for every teacher.	
Exemplars	*Nonexemplars*
1. Guided reading with the teacher takes place.	Students read when assignments are complete.
2. Students select books to read.	Students are assigned books to read.
3. Adolescent literature is used.	Lower grade texts are used for older, struggling readers
4. [vocabulary example]	
5. [fluency example]	
6. [comprehension example]	

handful, not a long laundry list. We want the list to actually be implemented.

You may be thinking that your reading intervention teachers would never think of doing the nonexemplars and every day would do the exemplars. This is something to celebrate, but it also means that the exemplars in the example may become your nonexemplars if they are typical practice. How would you kick each of those exemplars up a notch? Yes, you are refining and fine-tuning the expertise of your teachers. This also means that exemplars from school to school will differ, since the students in each school are different and faculty in each school are different. This is not a cookie-cutter list to be replicated at every school. Exemplars on the list model adult learning and identify clearly where the teachers are and where they should be as the year proceeds. Exemplar development in each school is a personal experience, and commitment on the part of the teachers in each content area is essential. That is why it is so powerful for improving student achievement.

When the group has a good understanding of exemplars, ask the participants to select a content area for development of exemplars and nonexemplars. All teachers in the group need not be teachers of that subject. In fact, those who teach other subjects may select to cross over to coach their peers! At a minimum, have groups develop exemplars for English or language arts, reading intervention, second language learning, special education, mathematics, science, social studies, vocational, electives or physical education, and library or media. Ask one member of each group to lead the process and select a spokesperson for sharing with the entire group. The groups should take about 10 minutes to develop five to six exemplars and nonexemplars. Post each set. Ask the spokesperson to share and explain each one. Discuss, clarify, and edit the exemplars and nonexemplars as needed. This is where it is valuable to have that knowledgeable facilitator who will recognize research-based strategies and will probe, question, and clarify what has been drafted. After each group has shared and revisions are made, the facilitator should ask, "Do you all commit to work toward these exemplars and reduce the use of nonexemplars?" This affirmation of commitment to action is a powerful closure to developing exemplars and nonexemplars.

Exemplars and Nonexemplars: The St. Lucie County Schools

When the exemplars and nonexemplars were developed for the St. Lucie County Schools, it was important for the collaborative team to think across grades, pre-kindergarten through 12th, and across a diverse district. Reflecting on how research-based practice across grade levels and content areas has similarities but differences also helped them to clarify what excellence was versus what was typical. Exemplars and nonexemplars were developed for the following categories:

- elementary reading
- elementary science, social studies, and mathematics
- English for speakers of other languages
- Middle and high school reading
- Middle and high school English
- Middle and high school science, social studies, and mathematics
- The media center

Let's look at the exemplars the team created, shown in Figure 4.2. From these examples, can you see the distinction between what is typically accepted and what kicking it up a notch looks like? What will happen to student achievement if every teacher moves from the right side of the figure to the left in daily practice?

Exemplars and Nonexemplars: Literacy Leadership Institute

On October 14, 2004, a nationally representative group of 77 educators participated in a seminar called the Literacy Leadership Institute, in Dallas, Texas. As part of the institute, the group generated exemplars and nonexemplars. Those for mathematics, science and special education are shown in Figure 4.3 on page 53.

STEP 5: CLARIFYING ROLES AND RESPONSIBILITIES

After agreeing on exemplars and nonexemplars, the faculty and LLT will be really pumped! They have been empowered to move from research to applications specific to their school and to their classrooms. For the first time in most of their careers, they are going to be asked what they need from administrators and colleagues to improve literacy learning. This is Step 5, clarifying roles and responsibilities related to literacy learning, which creates accountability in front of everyone.

Some of you are thinking, "Well, don't we all know what we're supposed to do?" Being explicit about roles and responsibilities related to literacy learning will provide new expectations for some faculty and staff. Although nonnegotiable expectations for daily practice have been created, along with exemplars and nonexemplars, some teachers

Figure 4.2 St. Lucie County Exemplars and Nonexemplars

Exemplars	*Nonexemplars*
Elementary reading	
Comfortable reading area	Book shelf with books
Print rich environment with student work	Decorated room
Whole group, small group, work stations, independent	Whole group or same work only
Assessments to inform instruction	Open book and read
Elementary mathematics, science, social studies	
Retelling, summarizing, making connections	Read chapter and answer questions
In student's own words, role play, explain	Writing facts and definitions
Nonfiction or informational text	Fiction or textbook only
Technology, supplementary text, other	Textbook only
Middle and high school reading	
Reader's theater	Read and play together
Book talks and literature circles	Computer quizzes
Themed books on varying levels	Class novel assignment
Student choice	Teacher-assigned reading
Student-owned strategies	Teacher-owned strategies
Continuous, daily modeling	Modeling one time
Reflective writing	Framed writing
Middle and high school English	
Post samples of student writing	Commercial posters
Student-generated question and answer, relationship	Textbook questions
Integrate vocabulary into reading and writing	Vocabulary lists
Student presentations (skits, drama, adaptations)	Movie with questions

(Continued)

Figure 4.2 (Continued)

Exemplars	*Nonexemplars*
Student-centered activity (literature circles, debates)	Chalk and talk (lecture)
Grammar games and activities	Overhead with examples and worksheets
Middle and high school content: Mathematics, science, social studies	
Use SQ3R[a]	Read the text
Student projects and teaching	Lecture, worksheets
High-level questioning	Low-level questions
Teacher-created labs	Canned labs
Assessing and teaching to student levels	Ignoring student levels
Relevant work and projects	

a. Survey, question, read, recite, review.

Used with permission of St. Lucie County Schools, Florida.

may still think they are not included in literacy learning—which we commonly call denial. Recently, a literacy coach shared with me (Rose) her excitement that the physical education teachers and athletic coaches had really jumped on their roles and responsibilities and were reading to students each day. These athletic coaches and physical educators were very pleased that their influence on students was recognized. She said with athletic coaches and physical educators leading the literacy learning charge, no one else had an excuse!

I've had principals say things like, "If you can help me with the media specialist, that would be great." When the faculty create roles and responsibilities for the media specialist, the pressure is taken off the principal, and no longer is the principal alone in encouraging change. Instead, there are 75 or so colleagues who have said, "Here is what I need from you to do my job better. Will you please help me with these things?" I have found that librarians and media specialists in many cases have to rethink their roles and responsibilities, from being the keepers and protectors of books to being the marketers of

Figure 4.3 Literacy Leadership Institute Exemplars and Nonexemplars

Exemplars	*Nonexemplars*
Science	
Select essential words; provide definition	Look up provided vocabulary words
Before and after use of graphic organizers	Lecture and independent note taking
Model, provide purpose, make connections	Assign chapter to be read in textbook
Ongoing assessment, authentic assessments	Unit tests
Mathematics	
Connect to history, life, and science	Use textbook only
Incorporate literature related to concepts	Tutorial software
Inconsiderate problems[a]	Commercial posters
Visual and concrete models	On-the-board work
Special Education	
Individual instruction	Whole-class instruction
Good literature	Drill and kill
Field trip and hands-on experiences	Read about only
Systematic strategy instruction	Assuming they know strategies
Teach higher level thinking (analysis, application, synthesis)	Teach knowledge and comprehension level only

a. These are challenging problems that cause students to think.

books to staff and students. Instead of focusing on quiet and inventory, why not have a little talking about books going on over a hot chocolate or lemonade? One literacy coach told us that if a teacher checked out a set of books to have in her classroom library during a particular unit and any books got lost, the teacher personally had to pay for the lost books. Such negative practice would inhibit any teacher from developing classroom libraries and from using the resources in the library.

After meeting with all of the media specialists in Lake County to develop deep understanding of literacy and strategies they could consider to influence student achievement, I (Rose) began to step into the media centers as I visited the schools the following semester and observed that changes were taking place. In South Lake High School, the media specialist ordered books of interest to adolescents as well as books on tape and developed a bulletin board of books recommended by students. The display contains photos of the students with their reason for recommending the books to their peers. Next to the bulletin board are the recommended books so that students and faculty have easy access without having to look for them. This enterprising media specialist is using adolescent peer influence (which is stronger than adult influence) to encourage reading and making it easy for students and faculty. The results of honest and forthright development of roles and responsibilities will be very positive and enhance reading, writing, and content learning in your school.

This process provides insight for administrators and faculty in many positions and requires a trusting, collegial relationship among the faculty. Although your LLT or faculty have just created exemplars, you are reinforcing exemplars with explicit sets of roles and responsibilities. In addition to those content area teachers identified in the exemplar strategy, you will want to think about all of those stakeholders who need clear direction related to literacy learning. This may include the Title I coordinator, parent liaison, resource teachers, curriculum specialists, parents, principal, assistant principals, substitutes, and paraprofessionals or teacher assistants. If the administrative team does not want to include themselves in this step, then I (Rose) would leave the step out altogether. You will gain quantum leaps in literacy learning if administrators have their own roles and responsibilities and then follow through on meeting those responsibilities.

Often schools will decide to create roles and responsibilities for district staff that support them and for district administrators. This is a proactive and positive way to say, "We included you in our fail-safe literacy system and we would like you to assist us in these ways." When the district literacy system in St. Lucie County, Florida, was initially facilitated, roles and responsibilities were developed for teachers, media specialists, literacy coaches, paraprofessionals, and school-based administrators. The collaborative team representing stakeholders across the district decided to add district roles and responsibilities, to send a strong message that everyone employed by the school district shares equally in student achievement. The kinds of items that emerge in the development of roles and responsibilities for district personnel tend to include

- providing funding for classroom libraries
- supporting teachers with professional development
- providing ongoing, teacher-friendly assessments
- providing easy-to-access data on individual and class reading achievement and growth
- being a guest reader for students

What district person would not want to support literacy learning? This invitation to participate will be appreciated by most district personnel.

Facilitating the Development of Roles and Responsibilities

By the time you get to Step 5, the faculty or LLT will be tired; they have worked hard throughout this process. They have been truly empowered. Make your list of positions (e.g., English and language arts teachers), not names (e.g., Rose Taylor), and put one on the top of each piece of chart paper. After you explain to the group that they will have 10 minutes to develop a list of roles and responsibilities related to literacy learning for these positions, invite someone to lead each of the groups. I (Rose) always try to ask different people each time to lead a group, to send the message that everyone is equal and everyone is a leader in literacy learning. Next, ask the participants to join whichever group they choose, and work for 10 minutes. At the end of 10 minutes, post the roles and responsibilities and have each group's representative share the roles and responsibilities. There will be discussion and clarification, allowing understanding. Some of the items may be edited. Since you are kicking learning up a notch and creating accountability, one professional to another, edits that create comfort but do not lessen expectations are encouraged. Sometimes, just wordsmithing makes a participant feel like a valued contributor.

There are those who question whether this step is wise. Will faculty create unreasonable roles for others? Will they use this step negatively against others? Honestly, I (Rose) can say that I have seen only positive results from this process. The synergy and collegial relationships that are fostered result in sincere, reasonable expectations between all participants.

At the national Literacy Leadership Institute in Dallas, roles and responsibilities for administrators were generated. Those that follow are selections from those created. Note that the majority of participants were either school-based or district administrators.

- Be highly visible.
- Be an educational change agent.
- Model literacy (support a print-rich environment, talk to students about reading and challenges, read as a guest reader).
- Interpret data and research.
- Foster productive conversations.
- Allocate funds and resources.
- Run defense against nay-sayers.
- Anticipate the next step.
- Do not blame—be a decision maker.

Roles and Responsibilities: *Just Read, Lake!*

In developing district pre-kindergarten through twelfth grade roles and responsibilities, the district team kept these general enough to apply but specific enough so that expectations and accountability were increased. Although in the facilitation of input, roles and responsibilities were identified for content teachers, reading intervention teachers, English and language arts teachers, and media specialists, the core group decided, for the published document, to fuse those groups into roles and responsibilities for teachers pre-kindergarten through twelfth grades. District leadership was also provided with input during the facilitation, and the team determined that leadership had received the message of what teachers and school-based administrators needed from them loudly and clearly. When the large, facilitated group reconvened to review and edit one last time, notice was taken and discussion took place of the synthesis of teacher positions' roles and responsibilities, including school-based (but not district) administrators and singling out the literacy coach. The group agreed that since the inception of the fail-safe literacy planning process, district administration had indeed stepped up to the plate and responded in a positive way to provide for and support school-based requests, and their responsiveness negated the need to include them specifically in the system. Since the position of literacy coach was new for every school, the team determined that it was politically important to clarify those roles and responsibilities also. Although librarians and media specialists are critical to improving literacy, the core team chose not to list them specifically in the literacy system but to encourage school-level literacy systems to do so, since their mode of operation and degree of friendliness to students and teachers varies from school to school.

The roles and responsibilities identified here were intended to provide a consistent foundation but not to limit commitment by any stakeholders in *Just Read, Lake!* School-level fail-safe literacy systems should be specific to content areas and other positions, to take this district expectation one level higher.

School-Level Administrators

- Be a literacy leader.
- Create a positive atmosphere and high expectations for literacy learning across all content areas.
- Analyze, organize, and disseminate student data.
- Take action using student achievement data.
- Ensure a scientific, research-based reading intervention for Level 1 and Level 2 (lowest) students, including appropriate personnel, professional development, materials, technology, and time.
- Ensure a systematic process that includes opportunities, participation, and follow-up of professional development.
- Participate in professional development with teachers.
- Support teachers in making instructional changes to improve literacy.
- Monitor instruction and provide feedback to teachers.
- Lead a literacy leadership team and develop a school literacy plan.

Teachers

- Develop teaching plans that reflect nonnegotiable expectations for daily practice.
- Implement nonnegotiables for daily practice.
- Participate in professional development.
- Communicate positively about literacy learning across content areas.
- Engage parents in literacy learning across content areas.
- Model the love of reading.

Literacy Coaches

- Model the seven processes of literacy and a love for reading.
- Design and provide professional development supporting *Just Read, Lake!*
- Assist the principal in leading the school literacy leadership team.
- Assist the principal in leading the development and implementation of a school literacy plan.

- Work closely with school administrators to keep them up to date on the literacy progress, success, and needs at the school.
- Maintain a professional library of literacy materials available for school use.
- Be willing and available to advise and assist teachers in assessing student needs and appropriate teaching strategies to improve skills.
- Actively promote the process of literacy in classrooms.
- Analyze student data to monitor literacy progress.
- Keep abreast of current scientifically based reading research.
- Engage parents and the community in the literacy process.
- Promote reading motivation program.
- Celebrate successes in literacy.

You will note in the administrator's list that there is a specific item related to the lowest performing students, those scoring in Levels 1 and 2 (below grade level) in reading. In reviewing the roles and responsibilities for school-based administrators, do you see a relationship to the four constructs identified in Chapter 1 (data-driven decision making, focus on continuous improvement of student achievement, leadership for change and innovation, and shared curriculum focus on standards)?

After reviewing these three sets of roles and responsibilities, is there any item on the list that applies to your position that you would not commit to? Do you believe that if all personnel in these positions were consistent with these behaviors that reading, writing, and content learning would improve? In Lake County, the district is counting on reading, writing, and content learning improving in a measurable way.

Action is following the development of these roles and responsibilities. At South Lake High School, Leesburg High School, and Umatilla Middle School, administrators conduct walk-throughs in classrooms every day, observing and reinforcing the daily non-negotiables and exemplary practice. They look for these in instructional plans and note them also. They are working closely with the literacy coaches to support school-based professional development and follow through in the classrooms.

Roles and Responsibilities: Sebastian River High School

Working with a school-level faculty to create roles and responsibilities is different than at the district level, where participants have varying experiences and perceptions of what is and should take place. A school faculty shares experiences, and at Sebastian River

High School, the positive school culture referenced earlier emerged in this step also. For purposes of example, you will find specific roles and responsibilities identified for categories of faculty: content teachers, vocational and electives teachers, English teacher, reading (intervention) teacher, media specialist, and administrative teams.

Principal and Administrators

- Be a leader of reading, a role model for students and staff.
- Put student literacy as first priority.
- Provide weekly updates on progress (strategy of the week).
- Provide professional development and materials for students.
- Support staff
- Celebrate accomplishments.
- $$$: Get funding from the superintendent!
- Create parent and community involvement.
- Outback [restaurant] night for all staff involved!

Content Teachers

- Use specific strategies for the content area.
- Guide students toward understanding standards through literacy strategies.
- Ignite student interest through variety of activities, multiple symbol systems, different ways of learning.
- Relate content to the student's world—connect to self, text, world.
- Use guest speakers, field trips, interdisciplinary projects.

Electives and Vocational Teachers

- Make materials applicable to other content areas.
- Integrate content into real-world careers
- Implement literacy strategies daily.
- Model the joy of reading.
- Accommodate students' needs.
- Provide equal access to standards-based curriculum.

English Teacher

- Connect reading, writing, and vocabulary.
- Involve students in a variety of ways of learning content.
- Structure learning, using literacy processes for success.
- Be a resource for other content areas.
- Foster, develop, promote, and celebrate the joy of reading.
- Teach students communication skills.

- Advise administrators and other appropriate personnel about materials we need to perform our roles.
- Communicate successful ideas with each other.

Reading Intervention Teacher

- Recommend age-appropriate materials and strategies for other teachers.
- Model exemplar reading strategies for other teachers.
- Assist teachers in the use of lexile levels (as you recall, the lexile system was defined in Chapter 1 as a system for identifying the reading comprehension level of students and of texts) in matching students' reading levels to texts.
- Bring back the joy of reading to the entire campus—students, teachers, staff.

Media Specialists

- Order appropriate materials.
- Obtain student and faculty requests (videos, audiobooks, etc.)
- Use lexile information (apply it to books).
- Provide accessibility to students.
- Provide access to reading support room.
- Do book talks focusing on a variety of young adult literature.
- Obtain audiotapes, if available, for all textbooks and other books.
- Provide bilingual books.
- Develop trunks of high-interest, low-reading-level books.
- Showcase pictures of teachers and students reading.

Since the development of these roles and responsibilities, the administrative team, faculty, and staff have taken them seriously. Administrators have found funding for new materials for those students reading below grade level. The media specialists have obtained new resources, have provided classroom libraries for all ninth grade English teachers, and say "I can't keep the books on the shelves!" Athletic coaches are actively involved in being role models. Each academy's team of teachers is developing a plan for how they will teach, model, and practice the strategies of expert readers and writers to the students in their learning community and how they will implement accountable independent reading. The ninth grade academy is finding success with these practices and in working as a small learning community to create consistency and support for every teacher in the academy.

When reviewing the English teacher and reading intervention teachers' roles and responsibilities, did you notice the request that they be resources to other teachers? This is very common among all faculties. The expectation that teachers in these positions be role models and support for teachers of other content classes puts positive pressure on them not only to implement daily nonnegotiables but to have deep understanding to the extent that they can assist others.

REVIEW AND REFLECTION

Creating a culture of trust is essential for this process to be successful. Trust the fail-safe literacy system planning process. Faculty will be fair to the principal and to their colleagues. They will also be honest in establishing what they believe is needed for learning to improve. Steps 4 and 5 are powerful for kicking learning up a notch and for creating accountability in a nonintimidating way for every member of the school community. Rather than teachers or staff being accountable to the principal only, they have agreed to be accountable to each other in the best interest of improving reading, writing, and content learning for all of their students. This accountability is supported with the action plan and support system that are created to make it all happen. Chapters 5–7 provide guidance in how to complete the fail-safe literacy system for your school or district.

HELPFUL TERMS

Exemplar: Exemplary, research-based behavior that is not common in the school. Implementing exemplars should improve student achievement.

Lexile: Numerical value assigned to a text related to the student's reading level.

Nonexemplar: Common practice or status quo practice in a school. Because it is common, continuing this same practice will not result in measurable improvement in student learning.

FURTHER READING AND RESOURCES

Taylor, R. T. (2002, December). Shaping the culture of learning communities. *Principal Leadership, 3*(4), 42–45.

Williams, R. D., & Taylor, R. T. (2003). *Leading with character to improve student achievement*. Chapel Hill, NC: Character Development.

5 Using Data to Drive Fail-Safe Literacy Learning

With a commitment to nonnegotiable expectations of daily practice in place and the creation of exemplars and nonexemplars to further guide classroom practice, the LLT is well on its way to developing a fail-safe system of literacy. As the LLT owns the research on literacy learning and how implementation of that research can make the daily work of every teacher easier, LLT members will be positive advocates for implementation. In fact, they may be so positive that they want to start creating a literacy system right away. Slowing down to look at the data on your students and teachers (with the research in mind) prior to developing the literacy system is important, because each school is unique.

STEP 6: ASKING WHAT IS WORKING AND WHAT IS NOT

Prior to asking the big question posed in Step 6, you will want to review school data from multiple perspectives and in the light of student and teacher subcategories.

First you will want to determine the categories of student data that are important. For instance, you will want to look at data by these groupings: first, grade level, class, gender, second language, special education, ethnicity, and free and reduced-fee lunch. Some of these categories may not be appropriate for your students, and you may have others to add. Until we know who we are succeeding with and who we are not succeeding with, we really cannot move forward with planning to assist in improving literacy or content learning. Generally, girls outperform boys in reading, and white boys outperform Hispanic and African American boys. All students may not require the same level of literacy learning; some may have emergency status.

Adairsville, Kentucky, has a kindergarten through eighth grade school. Former principal Mike Hurt charted student achievement data each year and documented gains. These gains were by school, by grade, and by classroom. He noted that there were teachers who consistently had greater gains than others and found it interesting that the teachers with the greatest gains attributed the gain to the students. Another point of interest was that the teachers who did not have the greatest gains also attributed their lack of gain and the gain of the other teachers to the students. With this observation, Mike strategically set expectations and provided appropriate professional development for faculty and interventions for those children who needed it most. These data-driven decisions (using both hard data and observational data) assisted Adairsville K–8 School in becoming a nationally recognized school for consistent growth in student achievement.

At Sebastian River High School, they know which students perform at what level, so they can intervene to the extent of the specific student's lack of literacy performance. The students all belong to an "academy" (a small learning community), and the administrators know which academies made the greatest gain and which made the least. By looking at achievement and growth based on class, teacher, team, or academy, a school can learn from the teachers and from the data whose students are growing the most. The administrators or literacy coach can also "coach up" the teachers whose students lack growth in reading or content learning.

An example of typical data-driven decision-making practice would be to compare fourth grade scores for 2004 with fourth grade achievement of 2005. What is wrong with this data analysis? The comparison is for different groups of students, who are assumed to be alike, but all teachers know that each year's group of students is decidedly different from the last, for a multitude of reasons. In contrast to comparing different years' students in the same grade level, track cohorts of students from one grade level to the next to determine whether the group is improving in their mean reading score. If the mean is not increasing each year, then there is a red flag for improving literacy learning. Improvement by one year is the expectation for all students. Students who read below grade level must grow each year by more than one year to close the achievement gap.

You will want to identify specific students in the quartiles or levels. Only when the data takes on faces and names does it have meaning for teachers. This level of data supports teachers in making informed instructional decisions and in monitoring growth or lack of growth. Many districts are creating online resources so that teachers and administrators can access individual student data relatively easily.

A word of caution: As you become more expert in data-driven decision making, keep in mind that data are more than state or nationally normed test results. Teacher grades, observations, attendance, attitude, discipline, and other data assist in creating a full picture of every student. I (Rose) recall when my son was in the fifth grade and testing came around the same day his grandmother passed away. Being a conscientious student, he insisted on attending school, as the teacher had emphasized how important it was to be present and do well on the Stanford 9 Achievement Test. During the testing, he became upset about the loss of his grandmother and did not finish the mathematics portion of the exam. Needless to say, if a judgment on his mathematical performance had been made on that single test, his academic career would have been less challenging than it turned out to be. This is an extreme example, but we must keep in mind that individual test data is one quick look on one day out of 180 days.

With the expectation of ongoing monitoring of student achievement throughout the school year, a principal can expect to have substantive discussions with teachers on a regular basis about group and individual student literacy development. Such data provide important information on teacher performance, as well as on student performance. Not only will you know which students are succeeding and which ones may need intensive immediate intervention, you will know which teachers need coaching and which ones need intensive immediate intervention.

One of the middle schools in my (Rose) community has a reputation for excellence. The principal began looking at the data, as we have suggested. What this novice principal recognized was that although the school mean for reading was high (70th percentile), there were still groups of students not meeting with success. As he began his second year as a principal, he invested in a reading software product, to be installed in the computer lab and to target the lowest 100 readers in the school in Grades 6–8. At the end of the school year, he wisely gathered data on the students who had participated in the reading lab experience to determine who it was working well for, so it could be modified or so the current year's success could be built upon.

What he learned surprised him. The principal found that the regular education students receiving no other reading intervention had a mean growth in reading of 1.2 years, on both the vendor's assessment and the state assessment. Special education students experienced less growth but still made gains in the seventh and eighth grades. Sixth grade special education students had a negative gain of .2. After substantive discussion, it was determined that perhaps the sixth grade special education students needed a different reading intervention for the following year, but for regular education students reading below grade level and for seventh and eighth grade special education students, the use of the reading lab would be continued. Note too that the students were also involved in accountable independent reading within the time scheduled into the reading lab.

Using achievement data on individuals, subgroups, and large groups of students is helpful in making decisions regarding such things as curriculum, instruction, materials, technology, professional development, assessment, parental involvement, and use of time within and beyond the school day. This type of data-driven decision making puts the principal and LLT on solid ground for scheduling, budgeting, and use of personnel to ensure improvement in reading, writing, and content learning, as well as preparing the principal and LLT for Step 6: Asking what is working and what is not working in literacy learning?

What Is Working and What Is Not Working in Literacy Learning?

With an understanding of the data on student (and perhaps teacher) performance under their belts, the LLT participants are ready to honestly consider what is working and what is not working in literacy learning. In most planning processes, it is recommended that the planning designees look at student achievement data and from that data design a plan for improvement. The fail-safe literacy system planning process diverts from hard-data-only decision making to honor the knowledge (data) of day-to-day experience in each unique school or district of what is working and what is not working in literacy learning. Those within an organization can tell the tale that is worth hearing and, after reviewing the disaggregated student achievement data, place it in the context of a school or district.

Why do you think we begin with *what is working* in literacy learning? Jot down what you think. Positive reinforcement yields more good performance, so it is important to know what is working. Acknowledging what is working will make teachers feel good about what they are doing and allow them to build upon it. Gathering data about what is working means that, rather than coming from a deficit perspective, teachers will be coming from a positive perspective of strength. Celebrate those successes! Those not doing "what is working" have the opportunity to learn and implement those behaviors. In this process, teachers often proudly note, "Hey, we're doing a lot of things really well!" The momentum to proceed and continue refining is there.

Additionally, when the LLT identifies what is working and then moves to what is not working, it may identify subsets of what is working. This goes deeper than would ordinarily happen in a planning process. Here is an example. LLTs often identify their motivational reading program as something that is working. Then, when asked, "What is not working?" they often say, "Well, our motivational reading program is not working for the lowest readers." This is honest and identifies not only who is not achieving satisfactorily but what is not working for them. An action item that might follow would be to maintain the motivational reading program for those for whom it works and add other dimensions for those not being reached. This type of deep-reaching action item is not identified in a process that only considers the data on student achievement and not the data on what is working for whom, in context. This context of the data is often in the minds of those who work with students every day.

We ask "What is not working?" to confirm the data and to learn what to refine or eliminate. When this question is asked out in the open, it is more difficult for teachers and administrators to continue unproductive practice. Following the identification of what is not working are *action items*. Going from data, to what is working, to what is not working, to action items is more beneficial than going from data to action items. The LLT has time to think through, acknowledge, celebrate, and commit to action this way, and it is personal. Data are impersonal, but what is working and what is not working is personal, because this is what teachers and administrators are doing!

A fail-safe system of literacy includes *curriculum* (advanced, average, two years below grade level, more than two years below grade level), *instruction, assessment* (diagnostic, monitoring, achievement), *materials and technology, professional development* (school and district), *intervention* (for those reading below grade level), and *parents and community*. Therefore, you will want to ask, "What is working in literacy learning?" and "What is not working in literacy learning?" in each of these categories. By doing so, you create an aligned curriculum system for literacy that works synergistically, rather than separate pieces and parts that may not have consistent philosophy and research. Creating this alignment results in an efficient and effective fail-safe system of literacy that simplifies the work of teachers and accountability for administrators.

Let's take each of the categories and review what a leader or facilitator would be looking and listening for. Examples are given from experiences that may emerge in the process. These are just examples. What emerges in any group is unique to that school and district community.

Curriculum

Curriculum should reflect alignment horizontally across the grade level with other content areas and vertically grade to grade. It should provide for accelerating the learning of all students: advanced, average, readers who are 1–2 years below grade level, and those who are reading more than two years below grade level. Alignment of the content of all sections of the same course or grade taught in a given school or district should be evident; otherwise, within the same school, gaps in learning become magnified. Aligning curriculum and making it accessible for all learners and their needs is critical to improving student achievement.

When the LLT at Sebastian River High School examined the curriculum in view of the school's students' reading levels, the team knew gaps existed that made accessibility to learning content standards a challenge. As a result, it created reading intervention for incoming ninth grade students who read at the lowest levels and another curriculum for those reading just below grade level. These two curricula support the successful curricula already in place for on-grade-level readers and advanced readers.

What is working? Curriculum appropriate for the reading level of the students.

What is not working? All students assigned to curriculum for on-grade-level readers.

Action item: Implement immediate curriculum intervention for the lowest level of ninth grade readers and a second tier curriculum intervention for those reading just below grade level.

Instruction

Instruction should be following the nonnegotiable expectations for daily practice. You may want to review Chapter 1, as well as the nonnegotiable expectations for daily practice and exemplars that your LLT developed. As an example of instruction at Sebastian River High School, I (Rose) was in a ninth grade science teacher's classroom that was print rich, with word walls and visuals. The students were preparing for a lab on mass and weight. The teacher led the students in developing a venn diagram on mass and weight, and when finished, she said, "and you can write a compare and contrast paragraph from this." As the students began to try to do the assignment, I asked the science teacher, "Have you ever modeled for the students or guided them in using the venn diagram to write a compare and contrast paragraph?" She responded that it had never occurred to her. "I'm not an English teacher. How would I do that?" I shared with her that all she had to do was go to the white board, pick up the marker, and tell the students that together they would develop the paragraph. Then she might ask, "What would be a good introductory sentence?" When she did this, the students began giving information and added sentences. Along the way, they discussed how to say things better. When it was over, in less than five minutes, she was convinced that the students could now all write a better paragraph with accurate information. Not only could they write a better paragraph, she believed that they had learned more science in the process. The next class period, she did it again, and at the end of the day, this science teacher was beaming and sharing with her colleagues what she had accomplished! Teachers will find that it works when they model, guide, and share in the learning. Students learn content, reading, and writing together.

What is working? Creating venn diagrams, followed by modeled and shared writing of compare and contrast paragraphs, in science.

What is not working? Assigning writing of compare and contrast paragraphs in science without modeling or shared writing prior to independent practice.

Action item: Model and share the process of comparing and contrasting, with graphic organizers, followed by shared writing; then ask students to write independently.

Here is another example of why it is important to ask "What is working and what is not working in literacy learning in instruction?" In an Algebra 1 class, the students were asked to do a warm up problem:

I'm traveling 625 miles to visit my aunt. I drive 65 miles per hour. How long will it take me?

Students quickly divided the 625 by 65 and came up with 9.6 hours. To their surprise (and mine), the teacher responded, "No, that isn't right. I want minutes." The teacher's error was in not being explicit when asking the question. She should have added, "Provide your answer in hours and minutes." She was actually wanting them to practice conversion from hours in decimals to minutes, but she never told them this. Clear, explicit directions work in literacy learning instruction.

What is working? Giving explicit directions and clarity in the question and the form expected in the answer.

What is not working? Unclear questions or questions lacking explicit expectations about the notation of the answer.

Action item: Teachers prepare questions and problems in advance to ensure clarity in the question and the expected notation of the answer.

The students were given another word problem to solve. They worked the problem but could not give the answer because they did not understand what was being asked. They came up with a number, but it did not answer the question. The algebra teacher asked the class, "Don't you all remember the steps I gave you?" No one answered in the affirmative.

I wrote on the white board:

Steps to solving a word problem

1. Read and understand the problem.
2. What is the problem asking?
3. What information do you need? Draw if you would like.
4. What information do you have?
5. What strategy will you use? Formula?
6. Work the problem.
7. Explain your answer.

The teacher agreed that steps 2 and 7 would remedy the most common challenges associated with reading and correctly solving mathematical problems. The students tried again, using these steps that included writing out their thinking, and were more successful. The next time I saw the algebra teacher, she affirmed that she was infusing literacy into her instruction, and the students' learning of algebra was going much better.

What is working? Posting steps for problem solving that include students writing out their thinking.

What is not working? Assigning problems assuming the students can read and understand the problem and what the problem is asking.

Action item: Post steps to problem solving. Check for understanding along the way. Ask students to follow the steps and write out their thinking.

Materials and Technology

When principals of districts invite me to visit in classrooms and be a personal trainer for literacy learning, I (Rose) always ask the teachers, "What do you want me to look for? What are your concerns?" Almost without exception they will say that their textbooks are boring, and they are trying to make them interesting but are having difficulty. They also say that the reading level of the textbook is too high for the students. Coincidentally, in two different locations, one in the East and one on the West Coast, I was handed two different science textbooks and asked to do an interesting read-aloud. Both times, I read and reread the chapters, looking for something that was written in an engaging manner. In both cases, a new vocabulary word was introduced in each paragraph, highlighted in red or blue, and accompanied by a few sentences of description. The chapters consisted mainly of terms and definitions, with a little expansion. Pictures and captions were the interesting parts of both chapters. I admitted defeat to both science teachers when it came to making the books interesting. After school, we discussed the need for concrete assets, and another science teacher said, "Look, a publisher's representative gave me this book as a door prize. It has exactly what you are talking about!" This door prize was *ScienceSaurus* (2002), published by Great Source. In contrast to the other textbooks being used, this book was clear, had visuals, and was written in an engaging and accessible way. We went on to discuss using *ScienceSaurus*, viable other options, and using the textbook as a resource only—after vocabulary, concept, and content learning had taken place. The current textbook alone was just too difficult for the students. As a result of this collaborative problem solving, the principal, a fail-safe literacy leader, purchased *ScienceSaurus* to be used as a supplement in the ninth grade science classes. The teachers were thrilled!

What is working? Labs, hands-on activities, interesting and accessible materials.

What is not working? Textbooks that are above the reading level of students and that are not engaging.

Action item: Teachers work together to create labs and to locate interesting, engaging supplementary materials. Teachers use the textbook as a resource.

We cannot overlook vocational and elective classrooms when considering literacy learning. In an auto mechanics classroom at Sebastian River High School, I (Rose) noticed that the textbook was explicit, with many excellent visuals and photographs. Every vocabulary word to be learned appeared to be supported visually. Not only was the textbook excellent, although the content was difficult, it was accompanied by a PowerPoint presentation for every chapter. When the teacher introduced the chapter, he told the young men to read the chapter, define the vocabulary, and answer the questions at the end of the chapter. After they finished, he planned to use the PowerPoint presentation to review and teach the students.

Within the classroom were about 12 students whose language was not English, and they were struggling with the assignment, although they were on task. Other students were having the same difficulty even though they were interested, motivated, and really wanted to learn about auto mechanics. In debriefing, I suggested that the teacher consider how excited the students got when he picked up an engine part and drew a relationship between the target vocabulary and that hunk of metal! Wouldn't it be better to use his excellent teaching skill by opening the class period with the PowerPoint presentation, pointing out the visuals, and drawing relationships to physical items in the classroom? He could follow the presentation by asking students to try to read the textbook, along with defining the vocabulary and answering the questions, if these were important. The teacher thought about it a minute and confirmed that it made sense, as most students could not read the textbook. Not only is it critical to have the correct materials and technology; it is also critical to use them in ways that provide all students with access to the content curriculum, such as beginning with listening, viewing, thinking, expressing through multiple symbol systems, *then* reading and writing.

What is working? Physical examples within the classroom; visuals; introducing concepts, vocabulary, and content through experience; then moving to texts that are on grade level or above.

What is not working? Assigning students texts above their grade level without introducing vocabulary, concepts, and content in other ways first.

Action item: Frame all instruction with before reading, during reading, and after reading strategies. Before reading, use visuals and physical examples to teach vocabulary, concepts, and content. Use the process of literacy in this general order: listening, viewing, speaking, thinking, multiple symbol systems, then reading and writing.

Those who are particularly interested in technology solutions for enhancing literacy learning will find Chapter 6 useful. In Chapter 6, the components of a literacy system are noted, with technology applications that schools indicate are working.

Assessment

What is working and what is not working in assessment related to literacy learning? Educators say the state test is working—and they say it is not working! Formal assessments for screening, diagnosing, and monitoring growth should be included. The facilitator should encourage the subgroup to think about classroom assessments as well as district- or state-mandated assessments. The group has more control over the classroom assessments. Participants may be allowed to vent their frustrations and feelings about certain items as long as the facilitator moves them to "What's next?" or "Is there an action item that you can think of that will improve the frustration?" At Mae Eanes Middle School in Alabama, the subgroup working on assessment had these kinds of items identified.

What's working? Alternative assessments, portfolios, projects.

What's not working? True-false, fill in the blank, and matching tests.

Action item: Professional development in classroom assessments, including authentic assessments.

In facilitating the development of *Just Read, Lake*! it became clear that the district needed to develop an assessment system that provided consistency among schools and could be tracked for monitoring improvement in Grades K–12. As a result of the fail-safe literacy system planning process, the district created a task group to design, train for, and implement a new assessment system for screening, diagnosing,

---

Examples from Sebastian River High School, Sebastian, Florida are used with permission.

and monitoring for the next school year. This represented commitment of time, personnel, and budget. Teachers and administrators can now access up-to-date information on students' achievement levels and use this information to inform instructional and curricular decisions.

Participants at the nationally representative Literacy Leadership Institute had other input for what is working and what is not working in literacy assessments.

What is working? Conferring with other professionals.

What is not working? Formal assessments do not always measure the objectives.

Action item: Ensure students have a variety of assessments.

What is working? Rubrics, observations, and checklists.

What is not working? Over-reliance on limited assessments such as end of chapter tests; lack of formative assessments.

Action item: Instruction driven by assessment and related to it; common grade-level assessments.

Professional Development

Districts and schools know the value of quality professional development. Districts frequently have a professional development plan that supports district goals and also have traditional offerings that have been in place over a number of years and may or may not be effective today. They could be good experiences and have value, but in an era of accountability, they may not be the offerings that will advance the schools and district toward the identified student achievement goal. The process of asking, "What is working and not working in literacy learning?" related to professional development will get at the heart of what teachers need and want so they can improve student achievement.

In facilitating the development of *Just Read, Lake*! common issues were raised. The district offered many excellent workshops, but teachers had to be out of school to attend. Additionally, many of the workshops did not have maximum attendance. The discussion came down to this: Offering the best experiences in the world does not improve student achievement. What makes the difference is when teachers participate in those experiences with follow-up at the school and coaching. After the LLT ended and the input was transcribed and studied, a smaller core team began honest discussion about professional development in the district.

These questions arose:

- Who attends these professional development experiences?
- Which of the five elements of reading do each address?
- What grade level teachers are the experiences targeting?
- Which of the nonnegotiable expectations of daily practice are addressed?

It took some time to review each of the offerings and answer these questions. As one might expect, the analysis yielded the answers that there were more offerings on some of the elements of reading than others and significantly more offerings for elementary teachers than for middle and high school teachers. Additionally, there was no data on who attended which experiences, as attendance was by teacher and administrator choice.

As a result of the input and follow-up analysis, it was determined that each professional development offering by the district would note the reading elements addressed, and more emphasis would be placed on experiences for teachers in upper grades. Furthermore, the data showed that professional development is most effective when schools do follow-up. Therefore an action item was to recommend a literacy coach for every school and the development of nine professional development modules (the Essential Core Professional Development Modules), to be delivered by those coaches in their respective schools at teacher convenience the following year. This provided a baseline of essential awareness and beginning knowledge for the implementation of *Just Read, Lake!* in every school. Regarding the need for follow-up and support: The administrators' roles and responsibilities identify follow-up and support after professional development experiences. You can see this in Figure 7.5, the leadership guide.

What is working? Professional development at the school during planning times or after school.

What is not working? Only professional development that is inconvenient or requires teachers to miss school.

Action item: (a) Recommend literacy coaches in each school, who will (b) create and deliver essential core professional development at each school.

Reading Intervention

Although reading intervention is not typically a component of a curriculum system, it is extremely important to invite honest perception and input if literacy learning is to improve. Students reading below grade level are, academically, the neediest of the students in the school, and it is worth inviting input from the LLT to refine service to this group. In my experience, there is no "typical" data generated from the LLT: It ranges from "teachers do their best in their classrooms" to "all Level 1 and Level 2 students are scheduled for 90 minutes of scientific, research-based intervention." Having said that, I do understand that most schools have some interventions that are working well, but many are short on funds to provide intensive intervention for all of those who have needs. By asking what is working in reading intervention and what is not working in reading intervention, the school or district gathers another set of data to take forward for appropriate resource requests. The example that follows occurred in a middle school in my community. By doing this analysis (along with data study), the school was able to support the teacher so she could improve the reading intervention for her students.

> *What is working?* Our software intervention for vocabulary and fluency.
>
> *What is not working?* Our software intervention does not adequately address comprehension.
>
> *Action item:* Teachers have accountable independent reading every day, and they teach, model, and practice strategies of expert readers and read to and with students every day to develop comprehension, in addition to continuing the use of intervention software for vocabulary and fluency development.

In another district literacy system, there was concern over the lack of consistency of quality intervention, but the district did not want to mandate a particular program. To address this issue, the following action item emerged:

> *What is working?* Intervention that is scientific and research based, with trained teachers.
>
> *What is not working?* Intervention with workbooks and untrained personnel.
>
> *Action item:* Intervention will have scientific, research-based curriculum, instruction, materials, and technology, along with appropriate personnel, professional development, and time.

In addition to being an action item, this statement appears under the responsibility of administrators. This action item and its inclusion in the administrator's roles and responsibilities *alone* should improve student achievement in reading.

Parent and Community Engagement

Engaging the parents and community in literacy learning can only add to the positive steps that educators take. All communities have a wealth of untapped resources in businesses, higher education, retirees, and stay-at-home parents. Generally, this component yields comments like, "Well, in elementary school the parents want to be involved, but as students get older, it is harder to have them involved." Actually, it may not be harder if we consider that this is about literacy learning—reading, writing, and content learning. Most parents of students of any age appreciate the invitation to participate in a substantive way in academic learning with their children, even if they do not have time within the school day to volunteer. Francis Catalon found himself principal of Crispus Attucks Middle School in one of the most challenging communities in Houston, Texas. Plagued by low student achievement, Catalon began his quest to turn the student achievement around, and he was wise enough to embrace the community and bring it into the school, as many of the adults had previously attended the school. He involved them to the extent that he set up a parent volunteer office in a school where you might not expect to find many parent volunteers. Over a three-year period, student achievement improved, and part of the credit goes to his substantive involvement of the families and the community.

District C in the Los Angeles Unified School District has many students living in poverty, great diversity, and families with second language learners. Guadelupe Simpson was the director of family involvement services and coordinated the family involvement specialists. With a vision of how these specialists could support literacy learning through their involvement with families, she began professional development on literacy learning for the specialists. They proceeded to develop learning events for parents and family members on literacy learning. These learning events supported the parents' literacy learning as well as their children's.

What is working? Targeted literacy learning opportunities for parents.

What is not working? General workshops on parenting.

Action item: Create and deliver strategic literacy learning workshops for parents.

In a recent district fail-safe literacy system planning session, there were parents present. They were pleased that this component was being addressed. Deep discussion ensued regarding ways to involve parents beyond the involvement of the early grades. The parents also emphasized the wealth of resources going virtually untapped in the retirement population. Here are a few of the items they generated.

What is working? Projects and assignments in which the student interacts with parents or community.

What is not working? Asking for donations or requests not of an academic nature, such as donating boxes of tissue.

Action item: Suggest to teachers that they include parents in their assignments. Example: Independent at-home reading log requires a parent's signature.

What is working? Automatic calling, messaging, e-mails, U.S. Postal Service.

What is not working? Flyers and notes sent home with students.

Action item: Budget for postage and incorporate technology for communication.

Facilitating Asking "What Is Working and What Is Not Working?"

As with the other steps, this one requires a comfort level and trust that participants will be able to identify what is working in literacy learning and what is not working. Prepare the charts in advance with the component at the top of each, with "What is working?" on one side and "What is not working?" on the other. I ask participants who have not led a group to take one of the charts, and I invite participants to work in the group that they prefer. About 10 minutes in the group is sufficient to generate initial input. Invite the groups to add either a third section for potential actions or, under each item of what is not working, write a potential action item in a different color so it will stand out. In generating what is working, what is not working, and potential action items, the LLT must think big across other departments and grades, if it is representing a school, or across different schools, if it is representing a district. This is, also, a solution-seeking process, not a process for blaming or whining. Leaving the decision making and final recommendations to the core team, probably the lead administrator and key teacher leaders, is a good idea. By this time

Figure 5.1 What's Working in Literacy Learning?

What's Working?	*What's Not Working?*
Assessment	
Projects, authentic work	Objective tests
Voluntary oral reading	Round robin reading
Action items: Assistance with assessment. Need classroom reading assessment to monitor reading improvement. Every teacher provides progress reports.	
Materials and technology	
Respectful materials for students who read at a lower level	Unattractive texts
Textbooks divided into smaller chunks	Texts above students' reading level
Action items: Purchase classroom computers and research-based software. Provide more time for students to use computer labs before school, after school, and on non-school time. Provide library access before, after, and during school time. Investigate texts with respectful content that are on reading levels of students.	
Parent and community engagement	
Parent personal contact (phone calls, conferences)	Bulletins carried home by students, PTA meetings
Action: Have grade level and team meetings for parents. Schedule meetings at least one month in advance. Provide parents with syllabi and tips for helping their students.Create an annual calendar of school-related events.	

Used with permission of Mae Eanes Middle School, Mobile, Alabama.

the LLT will be very tired, as members are likely to have been working together for about six hours and stopped only for brief breaks and lunch.

After each subgroup completes its input and posts it, a representative from each group will share the group's thinking. Other items or revisions can be made during this sharing. You will find that the LLT will be amazed at the doable action items they have identified and at the team spirit directed toward finding solutions for those not identified. In Figure 5.1 are excerpts from Mae Eanes Middle School's facilitated system planning.

STEP 7: ASKING IS THERE ANYTHING ELSE?

It is quite possible that there remain important issues or concerns that have not come to the surface. Ask, "Is there anything else that is important in developing your fail-safe literacy system that should be considered?" The input is charted at this time to ensure that it is not omitted in the writing of the system. Often there will be emphatic statements regarding budget priorities or perhaps the need for school-based professional development or specialized teachers or reading coaches. In Lake County, budgeting priorities to take to the board were interjected at this point that included funding literacy coaches at each school and a new assessment and data retrieval system.

When asked if there is anything else to consider, another common statement is, "These students are absent too much!" Yes, if the students or teachers do not come to school, student achievement suffers. An action item may be to target lowest achieving students with the lowest attendance for attendance improvement. This kind of input is essential to address in the school or district fail-safe literacy system. These items are captured even if they have been mentioned earlier in any of the other sections. Some may need extra emphasis. The LLT may choose to have an introductory or concluding section in the fail-safe literacy system entitled Budget Priorities or Action Priorities.

REVIEW AND REFLECTION

As I (Rose) have worked with school faculties and district collaborative teams using this fail-safe literacy system development process, I have found that participants really enjoy identifying what is working in literacy learning and what is not. Some of them have not felt free to acknowledge what has not been working and have felt great relief at being invited, in a safe environment, to put issues on the table. This type of collaboration empowers all participants to do their best thinking and put their best ideas on the table for consideration. Such collaboration reflects the true sense of a learning community, resulting in commitment to action.

These steps in developing a fail-safe system of literacy have brought you to a point of action. One of the common actions is the investigation of materials and technology that will accelerate literacy learning. Because this investigation is so common, Chapter 6: Enhancing Reading, Writing and Content Learning With Technology is included to provide you with support in thinking about research-based, appropriate technology integration. Then Chapter 7 concludes with ways in which to complete the fail-safe system of literacy with evaluation, enhancements, and celebrations.

complete the fail-safe system of literacy with evaluation, enhancements, and celebrations.

HELPFUL TERMS

Self-reflection: Thinking about my own professional work. What I am doing that is working? What do I need to do a little better? Where can I go for assistance?

FURTHER READING AND RESOURCES

Armstrong, T. (2003). *The multiple intelligences of reading and writing.* Alexandria, VA: ASCD.

Hurt, J. (2003). *Taming the standards: A common sense approach to higher student achievement, K–12.* Portsmouth, NH: Heinemann.

Lambert, L. (2003). *Leadership capacity for lasting school improvement.* Alexandria, VA: ASCD.

ScienceSaurus: A student handbook. (2002). Wilmington, MA: Great Source.

Smoker, M. (1996). *Results: The key to continuous school improvement.* Alexandria, VA: ASCD.

Smoker, M (2001). *The results fieldbook.* Alexandria, VA: ASCD.

6 Enhancing Reading, Writing, and Content Learning With Technology

In Chapters 1–5, you, your faculty, and your Literacy Leadership Team have been guided with research-based literacy learning and the fail-safe literacy system planning process, which is realistic and will make a measurable difference in reading, writing, and content learning when implemented, monitored, and revised. These measurable differences should be visible in teacher-given grades, reduced need for disciplinary measures, enhanced motivation, improved attendance of students and teachers, and (last but not least) improved scores on formalized testing.

With accountability on everyone's mind, administrators and teachers are seeking solutions that will accelerate reading, writing, and content learning. When you identify what is working and what is not working, it may be that some questions arise regarding materials and technology. Action items may emerge that require investigation of solutions that enhance and accelerate student literacy learning. A persistent inquiry from schools and districts is, "What do you recommend for technology purchases?" There is no one simple answer. In this chapter, Dr. Glenda A. Gunter, a specialist in instructional and curricular technology, will guide you with some queries to pose and some examples of technology integration that are consistent with the fail-safe literacy point of view and appear to meet the expectations for improving learning gains. Web sites will also be provided for your consideration.

When you are thinking of investing in a product, certain things will make your decision easier. For example, research should be available to clearly show how products have been designed to assist in the reading and writing process and how the results have been validated. In addition to the vendor's research, you may want to check out the potential purchases with the Metiri Group's Web site (www.metiri.com) for objective and unbiased research. This Web site investigates technology solutions and assesses them based on an evaluation rubric. Their Technology Solutions that Work database makes available an in-depth analysis of technology solutions created for K–12 education, and the Web site places the research at your fingertips. At the Web site, you can review detailed analyses of a variety of technology-based learning solutions and software. For more evaluation choices, you can subscribe to their services, at a very low yearly rate for multiple schools.

Also, we will discuss the significance of 21st-century skills and how they relate to your fail-safe literacy system. The potential of appropriate technology infusion into curriculum, instruction, assessment, and professional development will be shared, thus adding value to your fail-safe literacy system. In addition, devices that will aid productivity, leadership uses, and management of data for accountability purposes will be discussed. We are not advocates for any particular technology or software, but we do believe that appropriate technology integration can increase reading, writing, and content learning; therefore examples are provided.

21ST-CENTURY SKILLS

You are likely to be asking yourself, "What are these 21st-century skills, and why are they so important to literacy learning?" First, you must note that 21st-century skills are aligned with the fail-safe literacy point of view and should be integrated into standards-based instruction. The six elements of 21st-century skills are

- *Emphasize core subjects.* All 21st-century skills must be built into the core subjects as defined in the No Child Left Behind Act, including reading and language arts.

- *Emphasize learning skills.* Find ways to keep learning continual throughout students' lives, and motivate students to want to learn.
- *Use 21st-century tools to develop learning skills.* Use the digital tools that are essential to everyday life.
- *Teach and learn in a 21st-century context.* Teach using real-world, authentic examples.
- *Teach and learn 21st-century content.* Infuse technology into the curriculum.
- *Use 21st-century assessments that measure 21st-century skills.* Assessment should be effective and sustainable (Partnership for 21st Century Skills, 2003).

A quick glance at these skills brings a nod from all. Yes, literacy learning should access available, research-based technology; connect to the students' lives and the world beyond school; be infused throughout the school day; and use ongoing assessment to inform instruction. Technology has the potential to make all literacy learning easier and faster, with immediate feedback to students, teachers, and leadership.

The world in which our students live is significantly different from the past. Today's students use cell phones, pagers, instant messaging, personal desk assistants (PDAs), and laptops to connect to friends, family, and others in their community and all over the world. Our students now have at their fingertips a virtual world—with all its promises and pitfalls. Educational technology can be a valuable tool to achieve learning gains if it is integrated into the curriculum appropriately. Particularly when combined with the literacy non-negotiables, appropriate technology can help deliver significant and positive results.

WHAT IS TECHNOLOGY INTEGRATION?

Shelly, Cashman, Gunter, and Gunter (2004) state: "technology integration, also called curriculum integration is the combination of all technology parts, such as hardware and software, together with each subject-related area of curriculum to enhance learning" (p. 6.05). Therefore, technology integration includes the effective infusion of various technologies throughout the curriculum to help students achieve standards-based learning of each lesson, unit, or activity. Technology integration can be an integral part of fail-safe literacy planning when you look at what is working and what is not in instruction, materials and technology, and professional development.

Teale, Leu, Labbo, and Kinzer (2002) stated,

> Technology profoundly affects the learning and teaching of literacy, as well as the nature of literacy itself. It always has. The development of book technologies in the early 1500s set in motion the need for book literacies and many of the abilities we currently teach in our classrooms. Today, new literacies emerge as new technologies for information and communication demand new skills for their effective use. (¶1)

By supplying new avenues for learning, technology continues to open new opportunities for teaching students to be good readers and writers. Multimedia and digital media literacy programs combine software with print, audio, video, animations, visual materials, and manipulatives that provide teachers with an assortment of tools for incorporating the processes of literacy (reading, writing, speaking, listening, viewing, and expression through multiple symbol systems). Many of the programs are also supplemented with Web sites that not only extend the program but provide resources and access to those resources.

As you recall from Chapter 2, the five elements essential for developing good readers are phonics, phonemic awareness, vocabulary, fluency, and comprehension. Throughout this chapter, we are going to focus on those five elements and discuss the various technologies that can enhance the learning environment to create a fail-safe literacy system. Appropriate integration of technology in the curriculum can create an environment that promotes literacy learning throughout the school in all content areas and in all grade levels.

LITERACY LEADERSHIP AND TECHNOLOGY

To support the importance of technology and student achievement, technology integration is addressed in the No Child Left Behind Act. NCLB states,

> To encourage the effective integration of technology resources and systems with teacher training and curriculum development to establish research-based instructional methods that can be

> widely implemented as best practices by State educational agencies and local educational agencies. (¶13)

Leadership commitment to the funding and support of technology integration is demonstrated in the NCLB Act. The primary goal of this section of the NCLB Act is "to improve student academic achievement through the use of technology in elementary schools and secondary schools" (Part D, § 2402 [b][1]). The NCLB Act sets the stage for addressing the issue that schools are facing, which is leadership in the integration of technology to develop literacy for all students. A great document to help you understand and adhere to all the requirements of the NCLB Act is the *K-12 Principals Guide to No Child Left Behind* (National Association of Elementary School Principals & National Association of Secondary School Principals, 2003). The guide is written from the principal's perspective and is organized around important provisions of the law, accountability, staffing quality, sanctions and rewards, and curriculum and instruction.

As leaders, you are critical to the successful technology integration that will improve literacy learning. Gunter and Murphy (1997) conducted a study on the importance of administrative support in technology integration. Their findings revealed that administrator support played a key role in the acceptance and effective use of technology by teachers for instructional purposes. The research supported the idea that leadership from the principals played a vital role in the effective instructional use of computer technology and reiterated that the role of administrators is a key component for successful effective technology integration in literacy learning.

An example of leadership for technology integration and literacy learning can be seen in Principal Dr. Gladys White of Robert Hungerford Preparatory High School, which opened in fall 1999 and was Orange County, Florida's first magnet school of choice. When Dr. White became principal of Hungerford Prep, there was little technology in the school, and most faculty were brand new to both the school and teaching. One of her goals was to make sure teachers were trained to integrate technology to meet the content standards. She not only found funds to purchase technology, provide professional development that included hands-on workshops, and provide a graduate level course, but also, to show her support, she enrolled herself in the same courses and workshops and created projects along with her faculty. Her profound leadership has brought Hungerford Prep to its status as a high-performing school.

Technology Planning

Due to the enhanced attention to literacy accountability, leadership in the area of technology planning has also come to the forefront. In addition to your fail-safe literacy leadership system, there should be a sound, supportive technology plan. These plans should work hand in hand if learning gains are to be achieved. Most states and departments of education are looking for defined leadership prior to funding grants and other programs in the area of technology. A great place to locate sample technology plans, get advice from other leaders, and locate resources is the National Center for Technology Planning, located online at www.nctp.com. The level of achievement that a school has in integrating technology relies on the quality and commitment of the leadership to the technology plan. A good explanation of why technology planning is so important is described by the Regional Technology in Education Consortia's Technology Plan Task Force (2004) in their definition of technology planning:

> A technology plan serves as a bridge between traditional established standards and classroom practice. It articulates, organizes, and integrates the content and processes of education in a particular discipline with appropriate technologies. It facilitates multiple levels of policy and curriculum decision-making, especially in school districts, schools, and educational organizations that allow for supportive resource allocations. (¶1)

The technology plan provides a guide or a road map based on the mission of the school and the learning needs of its students. The plan should be continuous and focus on the purchasing of technologies, professional development, and evaluation of the effectiveness of the plan to meet the content curriculum standards. A sound technology plan interwoven with your fail-safe literacy system makes it possible to make the most of the potential of technology innovations while overcoming the challenges of implementation. The National Center for Education Statistics created a practical guide that provides tested approaches to obtaining, managing, and integrating technology in various educational environments. This guide can be found at the Forum Unified Education Technology Suite Web site (National Center for Education Statistics, 2005). The site helps individuals who lack extensive experience with technology to develop a better understanding of the terminology, concepts, and fundamental issues influencing technology planning and implementation decisions. Ultimately, it should result in wiser spending, improved literacy learning, and increased overall student achievement.

INTEGRATION OF TECHNOLOGY INTO THE FAIL-SAFE LITERACY SYSTEM

There are many new instructional strategies and innovative technologies that can enhance literacy. One of the first areas for technology integration to address is the literacy learning and content curriculum–specific learning. In the following, we address the components of your fail-safe literacy system of curriculum, instruction, assessment, and professional development and technology tools that may enhance your literacy system. We conclude the chapter with a discussion of technological devices that may assist literacy learning and data management.

Curriculum

Looking at the standards-based curriculum (what we teach) is the first and most important step in considering technology solutions. Many times, administrators, teachers, media specialists, other stakeholders, and the LLT can lose sight of the curriculum goals or individual student learning needs, because the technologies can be overwhelming and, at the same time, exciting. First and foremost, educators should remember that technology is only a tool to enhance or support curriculum-specific learning, such as reading. As with any tool, which technologies will be most appropriate depends on your school and your students. What is working and what is not working in the curriculum? Are there any content standards that your curriculum is not addressing? Are there technology solutions that teach standards more efficiently and effectively? By using technology in developing readers and writers, you are opening the door to opportunities that address other content standards, as well as introducing and teaching 21st-century skills.

For any technology tool to be used successfully, each user must be taught the proper use of the tool. Professional development will be discussed in more depth later in the chapter; however, we can say now that if teachers are not properly trained to use these technology tools, then we cannot expect to see effective technology integration that results in changes in literacy and student achievement.

Teachers should take steps to integrate technology into the entire spectrum of classroom experiences and find ways to use technology to teach literacy-specific content curriculum while showing students how technology can help them establish connections with themselves, other texts, and the real world. Always remember that the curriculum should drive the technology; the technology should not drive the curriculum. Which of the elements of reading or which of the nonnegotiables of daily practice does the technology enhance? This is where the research-based literacy solutions that target specific needs of specific students should be considered and become part of your fail-safe literacy system. Also, you should make sure the LLT is part of the selection, implementation, and evaluation of effectiveness of technology solutions for literacy learning.

When Jayne Ellspermann became the principal of Osceola Middle School, there was no technology in the school, no planning for technology, and no established professional development support for teachers. Her vision was to align the learning environment with the needs of the community; that is, provide an integrated learning environment. Students at Osceola Middle School were not reading at the level she thought they could. One of her first goals was to address the literacy learning curriculum by developing a Reading Literacy Lab. With her continual support, the lab was established and flourished. The lab contained 20 networked PC computers, using Compass reading software, with the purpose of addressing vocabulary and comprehension skills.

Great Leaps software, which addresses phonics, phonemic awareness, and fluency, was added to provide one-on-one direct instruction as a complement to the Compass software. Charts on student progress were provided for the elements of reading addressed by Great Leaps. To round out the system administrators, support staff and volunteers worked with the students individually on phonics, phonemic awareness, vocabulary, fluency, and comprehension. The technology proved to be the perfect mix, targeting specific learning needs and using personal professional intervention provided by a caring adult. Students came into the lab, signed in, and began working on the individualized lessons that the software program had generated based on the students' diagnostic assessment and performance.

Teachers were required to attend professional development and were assisted in attending conferences, such as the Florida Educational Technology Conference or Florida Reading Association Conference. Ellspermann encouraged grant writing and provided not only leadership in this area, but also help for the teachers in writing and submitting the grants. Literacy leadership is crucial if technology integration is to be successful and result in enhancements, curriculum projects, or classroom materials. Through her leadership,

Ellspermann enhanced the literacy curriculum, student achievement, and the capacity of the teachers at Osceola Middle School. Many of her teachers became so interested in learning more that they returned to local universities to gain higher education degrees in various areas of education.

Results revealed that the percentage of Osceola Middle School students scoring as proficient in reading according to the Florida Comprehensive Achievement Test improved from 54% in 2000 to 73% in 2003. Furthermore, the school improved from a state-given grade of C to A. As you can see, administrator support with technology integration led to measurable improvements in literacy learning.

Instruction

Let's look at some of the instructional technologies that have been shown to improve reading, writing, and content learning. There are a significant number of innovative electronic resources that have had an impact on literacy, so it is difficult to narrow them down to just a few. Teachers can and should use numerous kinds of technology to enhance student learning but should be strategic in using technologies for the purpose designed and within the environment researched. Using technology as part of a reading intervention can assist in meeting the unique needs of all learners. An excellent example is *Read 180,* an intervention program published by Scholastic, Inc. *Read 180* has very smart software that assesses and adjusts for each student based on spelling and comprehension, while at the same time providing students with immediate oral feedback and correctives. Developmentally appropriate, respectful software is offered for students in age-appropriate ranges. Such software engages students today who learn differently than those who become good readers with typical classroom instruction by Grade 3—and technology may offer different paths to engage these students and motivate them to learn. *Read 180* is unique, as it reflects the nonnegotiables of daily practice with print materials and incorporates software into a balanced literacy classroom, rather than relying on software alone for all of the literacy learning needs. *Read 180* represents an intervention fail-safe literacy system, when it is implemented as it was designed and validated.

Another facet of using instructional technology is the way research-based products can aid in targeting instruction on the five elements of reading depending on the unique needs of individual students versus an entire class or group. Technologies run the gamut, from simple technologies (focusing on phonics and phonemic awareness) that are currently available and found in most schools and classrooms to the most complex systems, created, like *Read 180* or *Fast Forward* (published by Scientific Learning), to assist in literacy learning.

One readily available technology, which has revolutionary instructional benefits for literacy learning, is hypertext. Hypertext, extensively used on the World Wide Web and in many software packages, provides an incredible advantage. Note that hypertext incorporates the literacy process of reading, listening, and viewing, which should lead to thinking and writing. Hypertext has the power to read highlighted text out loud or color code text, present graphics to help explain the text, provide definitions of words orally or in print, and even supply additional information about a topic. This can be critical for English oral support needed for the struggling reader or English language learner. Furthermore, animation can be added to the hypertext to gain the reader's attention.

Technology can be used to promote successful reading for students with varying reading levels by providing teachers with a variety of instructional options and strategies that are particularly helpful to struggling readers. A few resources that can provide a significant impact on literacy are talking word processors, e-books, e-book readers and software programs, and reading development tools.

Talking word processors are software programs for struggling readers, special needs students, and English language learners, providing text-to-speech capabilities for these students by assisting them with phonics and phonemic awareness, as well as vocabulary and fluency. Each letter and word is echoed back to the student as it is typed on the computer. Many of these software programs have reading literacy tools that promote literacy development. A number of reading development tools improve language skills, such as letter identification, word patterns, rhyming, and early sound-to-letter associations; others are literacy tools that concentrate on comprehension skills. There are also software programs that work on a specific area of reading, such as decoding skills, phonics, or sounding out words. *Simon S.I.O.–Sounds It Out* and *Write: Outloud* by Don Johnson Products and *Clicker5* by Crick Software are good examples of available software that provide immediate feedback to the student to assist with both reading and writing skills. Words can be highlighted or the text can be enlarged to assist a visual learner or a student with a visual impairment. All of these solutions are excellent for struggling readers, special needs students, and English language learners.

Electronic books (e-books) are digital books that can be downloaded to small, book-sized computers or any size computer that can hold thousands of pages of text and small graphics. E-book readers are hardware used to view e-books with enhancements such as music, simulation, animation, and sound effects. E-book readers also allow the user to read, save, highlight, bookmark, use dictionaries, and add notes to the digital text. E-books are very popular because of their portability. There are additional tools that will let you create your own e-books. One of these tools, created for the Palm handheld device, is *DropBox*, and it is free. Another really good e-book creation tool that is easier to use and is reasonably priced is Palm Reader. Using Palm Reader, students can create their own stories, or teachers can create stories for the students and use the program to assess students' comprehension of the reading material.

To support literacy, there should be a balance of these elements: guided reading, shared reading, interactive writing, and shared writing. These and many other technologies and Web sites can assist the teacher in enhancing all these elements. There are software programs, such as *Kidspiration,* Riverdeep *Destination Reading,* and Edmark's *Make a Story* series, and Web sites, such as www.starfall.com, for young readers, with audio output that will sound out the letters phonically, read words or stories, or let the student read or have guided reading. Additionally, students can click on hypertext words or graphics to access a dictionary or thesaurus.

The instructional technologies that you integrate into your system to improve reading, writing, and content learning can be those technologies that are readily available. The key is finding the best solution for each student that is strategic for the teaching target. An example may be using something as simple as the computer for word processing for all students; this has been shown to support the connection between reading and writing instruction. Students who use word processing to create their writing tend to have higher grades than those who write, revise, erase, and edit with pen or pencil. Word processing is an excellent way of letting students have hands-on experiences. Time after time, studies have shown that students read and write more when they have the opportunity to create and edit their work on the computer.

We know that assisting all students in owning the strategies of expert readers and writers is one of the nonnegotiables of daily practice. Software such as *Inspiration* and *Kidspiration* (Inspiration Software, Inc.) is easily used by students and teachers alike. Such software assists students in developing cognitive, concept, and vocabulary maps. Organizing information in a way that makes sense for learning vocabulary and content, as well as for prewriting, is an instructional asset for any classroom.

As we close this brief section on instruction, it should be apparent that the media center and media specialist have a critical role in providing access to appropriate technology solutions for teachers and students. Media centers, depending on their literacy focus and technology resources, can directly affect student achievement. As an example, in Florida, the high schools that scored in the top third on the FCAT given to all tenth grade students had 50% more computers in their media centers, and 42% more of the media center computers were connected to the Internet, compared with lower scoring high schools.

Interactive Media and Video Instruction

Interactive media is the language of students today. In the *Digital Divide Network*, Paula Monsef (2002) stated, "Students who may not take to learning by reading a textbook or listening to a lecture often jump at the chance to understand complex concepts by presenting finished products in the form of a film or a Web documentary or a PowerPoint presentation" (¶5). As educators, we have been using instructional videos for years; however, with the evolution of digital video technology and broadband Internet access, the ways in which standard-based instructional videos and other technologies can be used in the classroom have been revolutionized. Publishers acknowledge that textbooks are no longer the only instructional resource for successful teaching of a standards-based curriculum. Therefore they have responded by publishing CDs and DVDs and providing Web sites that are companions to the print resources. In today's classroom, videos, Web sites with multimedia enhancements, and DVDs should be incorporated to provide access to on-grade-level content curricula while reading and writing are developing in the content area.

Because of increased accountability mandated by the NCLB Act, you may be wondering whether research exists that shows how video can improve students' achievement. United Learning, a division of Discover Learning, an educational audiovisual and video content provider, conducted a study consisting of 2000 elementary and middle school students and 53 teachers from three rural Virginia school districts. United Learning compared streaming video with traditional learning instruction and found an increase in student achievement of 12.6% (United Learning, 2004). Reed (2001) defines video streaming as a "process of viewing video over the Internet." Video streaming allows users to simultaneously download and view a file without leaving any of those files on their computer. Video streaming allows educators to offer various instructional resources for a significantly reduced cost but with extremely high benefits for literacy. Recall that viewing is one of the processes of literacy that provides support for development of vocabulary, fluency, and comprehension of related printed text, particularly when introduced prior to print. A caution—*support* should not be misinterpreted to mean that teachers should use videos in lieu of sound instructional technologies or as rewards or time fillers. Videos should be used only as deliberate, purposeful instructional support.

Dr. Lynell Burmark (2004), author of *Visual Literacy: Learn to See, See to Learn* (ASCD), states, "Researchers have found that humans process visual information 60,000 times faster than text. And that visual aids can improve learning by up to 400 percent" (Nugent, 1982; Burmark, 2004). Video streaming and "on demand" capabilities have changed how we view videos and how we can use videos for literacy. Language arts teachers can implement innovative teaching strategies and integrate technology into their classroom using various videos along with literacy strategies. Researchers are reporting that when teachers use videos in guided reading groups, they find that students' retention of content and comprehension improves. Note that these experiences use the processes of literacy (reading, writing, listening, viewing, and thinking) to develop vocabulary, concepts, and content.

In using Robert Doman's (1984) concept of teaching to students' strengths and remediating their weaknesses, it is clear that you cannot always teach a student to read by simply giving him or her another book, especially if text-based communication is that student's weakness. Many teachers have found ways to get students involved by putting cameras and editing equipment in their hands. Most teachers are now having their students use digital cameras, camcorders, and other electronic media to create interactive Web projects and PowerPoint presentations, as well as video for multimedia interactive digital media projects. Multimedia and interactive digital media projects that are effective incorporate all of the literacy processes (reading, writing, listening, speaking, viewing, thinking, and communication through multiple symbol systems) and therefore give all students access to on-grade-level content, as well as developing comprehension.

The students in Brandi Evans's fifth grade classroom at Sabal Point Elementary in Longwood, Florida, have been creating digital media and video productions for more than a year. Last year, students worked on reading comprehension while conducting their research.

Students created videos by writing the scripts, creating the productions, and editing the videos for topics such as Great Women in History, the Johnstown Flood, and Leaders of World War II. Their latest literacy project was on the recent presidential election. Ms. Evans says students' literacy skills have improved. Students are motivated to read and complete assignments when the final outcome is doing something that they enjoy instead of another test. Using digital video and other media allows students to incorporate the literacy processes—reading, writing, listening, and speaking—into every assignment while learning standards-based content. To write scripts, students have to retell events and facts in a logical and sequential manner, as well as summarizing and synthesizing facts from various sources—key indicators of comprehension. Students gain fluency as they rehearse, edit, and begin to perform their scripts. Students are able to self-correct because they can see and hear mistakes that they might not have caught if they read their scripts alone. Teachers also benefit from student-created video because teachers are no longer assessing students' recall of obscure facts. They can see where students' misconceptions are as students begin to write and perform, and this perspective supports the teacher in knowing when immediate clarification or intervention is necessary.

Assessment

Ongoing assessment is a requirement of accountability. As a leader held accountable for growth in reading, you cannot wait for an annual assessment to know if the teacher's instruction is making a measurable improvement. When you consider instructional software purchases, you will want to have assurance that ongoing reports of student growth are easily accessible to the student, to the teacher, to you, and to the parents. You would be wise to investigate assessments that are teacher friendly and work with all subsections of the student population and all components of your fail-safe literacy system. As an example, Sebastian River High School has incorporated the *Scholastic Reading Inventory* (SRI) for pre- and postassessment of all students. This same assessment is built into Sebastian River's first-level intervention, *Read 180*, and into the second level of intervention, *Read XL*. For motivating independent reading, the school has implemented *Reading Counts*, which also uses the SRI to measure growth and to assist teachers and media specialists in matching students to text for accountable independent reading. Although just one of the multiple assessments the school uses, the SRI is a teacher-friendly assessment that runs throughout the school and across grade levels and achievement levels. You will want to investigate assessment software that can serve your students, teachers, and parents in a manner that is systematic and easy to use.

Many software programs and systems offer a way to track student achievement and progress on teacher-given assignments. Some technology projects that students create are not as easy to assess; however, rubrics are a great way for teachers to evaluate students' work. Rubrics are a way of showing how each component of a project is aligned with the standards. Rubrics show to what extent students mastered each component of a project. Several rubric generators, such as RubiStar.4teachers.org and Teach-nology.com, are available to educators free of charge.

Professional Development

Throughout this chapter, you have seen many technologies that can assist in the literacy process. The procedure of implementing technology can be less complicated and expensive than you think. However, you know your teachers need training. Professional development is a key component of a fail-safe literacy system that will be addressed in Chapter 7. Domine (2002) stated,

> Tremendous pressure still exists for teachers to learn how to use new technologies in some meaningful way, yet according to a report to the President on the use of technology in education, the network of support does not necessarily exist for teachers to integrate technology in ways that support school curricula. (¶1)

Appropriate technology integration can enhance learning; however, it must be supported by your leadership. To add to the fail-safe literacy system, leadership must create opportunities for teachers to develop new instructional strategies for literacy that include various technologies.

Many times, when educators plan for technology integration, professional development is thought of as an afternoon or all-day workshop or a couple of sessions on how to use a computer. For your fail-safe literacy system to be successful, professional development should be a priority and rethought to include a combination of instructional technology strategies for teachers, the media specialist, and all school personnel. All learning experiences should be focused, continual, and sustained. There should be practices that assist teachers in understanding how technologies affect them personally, professionally, and pedagogically. For example, experiences need to be real and focused on the needs of the teachers, their students, and the curriculum. Teachers need to see a way in which they can take the technology back to their classroom and apply it immediately, or they will not be interested in implementing and continuing to work with the technology. Teachers need to collaborate, meet, and discuss what they learned and chart out specific curricular goals; what strategies will support those goals; and, finally, what technologies will best support these strategies. For successful integration of technology in the literacy process, the school structure must support the teachers through the entire process of technology integration. Gunter and Sivo (2003) concluded, "The increase in purchasing technology at many of our nation's public schools has not improved student achievement. The primary reason is a lack of effective professional development and teacher training."

In addition to professional development for appropriate and effective use of technology, technology provides new resources for professional development. There are many examples, but many of the professional organizations—the International Reading Association, the Association for Curriculum and Supervision Development, and the National Middle School Association—offer online or Web-based literacy-related professional development opportunities. There are many other private industry providers of technology-based literacy professional development, as well as education-based providers, such as Florida On-line Reading Professional Development (FORPD), whose Web site is at www.itrc.ucf.edu/forpd/ and is free to all teachers in Florida; the program may also be taken for university credit, with appropriate acceptance. FORPD includes a teacher leadership module and an administrative leadership module for literacy. These technology-based opportunities for literacy professional development are only a sampling, so check with your local or state department of education to learn what is available for your teachers.

TECHNOLOGICAL DEVICES

What has truly changed the landscape of technology integration is the accessibility, portability, and wireless capabilities of technology. We now have so many options that make it possible to put technology in the hands of all students. Notebook or laptop computers, PDAs or handhelds, Tablet PCs, Alphasmarts, Danas, e-books, and many more portable technologies are making it possible to put the technology in the hands of students so they can read and learn anywhere, anytime.

Notebook Computers

A notebook computer, also called a laptop computer, is a portable, individual computer small enough to fit on your lap. These computers continue to get smaller, thinner, and more lightweight, yet they are as powerful as desktop computers. Many educators have reported being afraid of using notebook computers in the classroom, as well as other portable devices, due to security issues. In talking to many principals across the country who have implemented notebook or laptop initiatives, we have learned that they have seen a great sense of pride from the students. Actually, students were very protective of the equipment and took amazing care of the computers. Notebooks are a more expensive solution than desktop computers; on the other hand, prices have come down significantly. Additionally, notebook computers are easier to store and are completely mobile.

Notebooks give the students more flexibility and mobility in the classroom. For example, if the notebooks are part of a wireless mobile teaching lab, also called a computer lab on wheels, teachers can share the technology and bring the technology to their classroom instead of taking students to the technology. This makes the technology a very flexible solution. Different types of software can be loaded to meet the needs of students and teachers. An excellent way to use this technology is having a "reading and writing center on wheels." When you have 30 students in a classroom, you really would like each of them to be able to work on the computer, but few teachers have more than three to five computers available, and many still have only one in their classroom. Wireless mobile labs can be purchased in sets of 10, 16, 24, and 36 computers. With a mobile lab, you are putting the technology in the hands of the students and in the classroom when it is needed. Plus, a mobile lab can be shared among teachers—just roll the lab to the next classroom. We know that not every minute of every student's day is spent on the computer, so why not have a solution that is adaptable?

Handheld Solutions

PDAs, personal information managers, and handhelds are mobile, wireless devices or computers that fit in the palm of your hand. Handheld devices offer a solution to access and equity issues; however, they are so much more to education: They combine the power of technology with the convenience and low cost of small portable devices. Handhelds provide the opportunity for each student to have access to technology on a one-to-one ratio. Also, they can be a collaborative tool in the classroom. Although handhelds cannot substitute for many other types of technology, they can assist in meeting individual literacy learning and teaching needs.

In regard to data management, many software applications are available for handhelds that score, analyze, and document student reading performance. There are reading assessment tools matched to literacy standards or individual student or entire class reading report generators. These tools can track teacher observation assessments, store and track student individual education plans, and more. In addition, there is dedicated software that allows assessment information to be uploaded to a Web site where the results are interpreted to determine whether students are mastering the five essential components of reading. One company providing this type of platform is Wireless Generation, which calls its mobile classroom assessment mCLASS.

Handheld applications for teaching are becoming endless. New software and additional devices are being developed for PDAs. Some teaching applications for handhelds are free of charge, and many more advanced applications can be purchased for a reasonable cost, such as applications for word processing, testing, and gaming; story writers; literacy lesson plans; multimedia tools for adding visuals, audio, and video; graphic organizers; and applications for Web clipping, with which students can download and read their research anytime. Teachers can create their own literacy games, concept maps, vocabulary lists, and electronic books to use in teaching vocabulary, content, and comprehension across curricula. Several enhancements available include attachable keyboards, screen-writing styli, science probes, global positioning satellite connections, digital cameras, digital video cameras, digital audio recorders, audio output devices, and Presenter-To-Go, which connects your PDA to your projection system and makes the PDA a handheld teaching computer.

Students can read text on the PDA, have the text read to them, click to get definitions and find graphics and multimedia enhancements for viewing and listening skills, be supplied with cues that can help them develop fluency in their reading, and be assessed on their comprehension of the content—all in the palm of their hands. Note that this type of technology support gives access to on-grade-level text and content for those students not reading on grade level and for

English language learners that they would not otherwise have, while at the same time developing literacy. Handhelds have a great deal to offer in the area of literacy because of the amazing capabilities of the literacy software available, much of which is free or economically priced. Plus, the flexibility and portability of the devices add to the possibilities for learning.

K–12 Handhelds, Inc., a company whose mission is to educate and train administrators and teachers on handheld devices, has unlimited resources concerning the use of handhelds in the school. Their Web site, www.k12handhelds.com, has many resources for administrators and teachers of all grade levels. Ongoing research is being conducted by SEIR-TEC of SERVE and Florida's Instructional Technology Resource Center, in conjunction with K–12 Handhelds, on the use of handhelds to improve reading literacy skills. Their results, recommendations, and resources are available at several Web sites: www.seirtec.org, www.itrc.ucf.edu, and www.serve.org.

Tablet PC

The Tablet PC is an ideal tool for today's classroom and today's students. The Tablet PC is designed as a compact, wireless, mobile computer that combines the benefits of a notebook computer and a writing pad. The Tablet PC contains features such as enhanced handwriting recognition and voice recognition, and it combines writing software with the power of a computer by combining functions such as voice and handwriting recognition. The design and versatility for learning has initiated thinking that this is the computer that will replace all the rest.

You can choose one of several different ways to use the Tablet PC. The tablet is the main part of the computer, and you can either connect a keyboard for easy typing or disconnect it so you can use the tablet computer like "intelligent paper," using a stylus writing tool that functions like a mouse and a writing pen. The screen orientation can be switched in seconds from portrait to landscape (lengthwise). Students can read text easily and at the same time do something they rarely are allowed to do with textbooks: They can mark, highlight, create drawings in the text, use audio to read the text, and more. This supports students who struggle with note taking by letting them highlight, underline, and mark text for meaning. These types of tools have led to quite a few companies (e.g., Holt, Rinehart, and Winston) creating electronic content for the Tablet PC. Holt, Rinehart and Winston is a publisher of textbooks and educational materials. The theory is that students can read anywhere, anytime, and anyplace and can make notes within the text to assist in comprehension of content. The president of Holt, Judy Fowler, stated:

> The Tablet PC is a compelling new platform for education. It widens the possibilities for technology-based interactive learning, enabling student access to an entire curriculum from a single, light, portable device. Holt Online Learning products delivered through the Tablet PC and Microsoft's Class Server 3.0 learning management platform, provide students with enhanced learning opportunities and the ability to interact with instructional materials in ways that previous platforms have not allowed. (Microsoft, 2003, ¶7)

A disadvantage of the Tablet PC is that because the product is new, the price is not comparable to desktop or notebook computers. However, with the advent of more manufactures and software being developed for this platform, the price is already starting to come down. This will be a very versatile tool for students.

AlphaSmart and Dana

The AlphaSmart and Dana are very economical computer devices that are durable and versatile and that make it possible to put a computer in the hands of every student at a very low cost. The AlphaSmart, a portable word processor, allows students to write, take notes, practice keyboarding, transfer files into any application on any computer, and print to most printers. For several years, teachers have been using the AlphaSmart in their classrooms to increase literacy. There are software programs with interactive reading and pronunciation instruction that can be loaded on the AlphaSmart and other devices to assist in reading, listening, and writing. Students can type letters and words, take notes, use spoken and written input, and then transfer those files to other computer devices.

Here is an example of using the AlphaSmart for the art of creative writing. Teachers can use the "hot potato" technique with students writing stories. Each student starts creative writing on his or her AlphaSmart. When time is called, each passes the AlphaSmart to the next student, and that student continues writing the piece started on that AlphaSmart. Switching continues, and interesting, authentic pieces are created. Additionally, students can label sentences using the AlphaSmarts to determine the different parts of sentences or parts of speech (e.g., subject, predicate, noun, verb, adjective) and use different colors to show the different parts.

New to the AlphaSmart product line is the Dana, which is a unique device that can be an excellent alternative to a laptop. This product has the affordability of a handheld but combines many of the features found on a laptop. The Dana uses the Palm OS operating system, giving students and teachers access to almost all Palm applications, but the device also has a full-size keyboard and a larger screen for viewing. Also, students can type or write, using a special stylus, directly on the screen. All devices listed can be used in the same way and also in many various ways to increase literacy.

THE INTERNET AND THE WORLD WIDE WEB

This section could be an entire book by itself, but we will highlight just a few of the unlimited possibilities that the Internet and the World Wide Web can assist in your fail-safe literacy system. Douglas Rushkoff (1996) stated perfectly, "Students are natives to cyberspace, where the rest of us are immigrants." Today's students are growing up with amazing access to information, people, ideas, and resources through a highly interactive media. The Internet and Web have large amounts of information available, and we know how wonderful it is for students to do research. While students are on the Web, they also are reading! There are an amazing number of sites dedicated to teaching literacy, many with all five elements of literacy and some with a particular emphasis, such as vocabulary or phonics. The best news is that many are free and well researched! At the same time that they are using these sites, students are learning information literacy, which means weeding through the information to find exactly the research or information they need to complete comprehensive projects that engage them in authentic learning experiences. Teaching these skills also places learning under the context of 21st-century skills.

Debbie Davis, principal of First United Methodist School, Kissimmee, Florida, decided that if she was going to try to get her teachers to adopt technology, she needed to learn something about technology herself, so she enrolled in a certificate program in educational technology. After learning what a difference technology could make in student learning, and wanting to change the way students in her school were performing in reading and writing, Davis became an advocate for curriculum integration. She decided that the best way to get the teachers involved was to use the technology itself to teach the teachers. She thought about ways to hook her teachers on technology, and finally put them in the learner's seat and created a WebQuest for her teachers' next professional development session. Bernie Dodge (1997), the creator of the WebQuest model, defined it as "an inquiry-oriented activity in which some or all of the information that learners interact with comes from resources on the Internet" (¶2). WebQuests can be used for activities, short lessons, reinforcement, introducing content, or for long-term activities and lessons. WebQuests are excellent ways for teachers to create inquiry-based reading, writing and literacy projects for students.

Because it was close to Thanksgiving, Debbie Davis decided to create a lesson based on the Pilgrims or English Separatists. Teachers had hands-on experience on the value of using the Internet in a lesson and the amazing content that could be used to create an interactive lesson. What made this principal so different was that she put herself in the learner's seat and created something in a format that she knew teachers would embrace. Using WebQuest can improve research skills and develop comprehension of content.

Another simple way to work on literacy is creating Scavenger Hunts. You supply the questions and students have to find the answers by visiting teacher-evaluated Web sites linked on a teacher-created curriculum page. A curriculum page is a teacher-created document or Web page that contains hyperlinks to teacher-evaluated Web sites that aid in teaching curriculum-specific content. Teachers can develop curriculum pages on any content. This is a super tool for teaching students to search for good information and not surf the Web. Also, by creating curriculum pages, teachers give themselves control over the content of the lesson and students' exploration of the Web. For example, you could use Internet sites such as the Merriam-Webster Online Dictionary. A student can click on a word, read the definition, learn more about it, and hear it pronounced.

REVIEW AND REFLECTION

Technology integration holds promise for enhancing literacy learning and accelerating reading, writing, and content learning. We began this chapter with emphasis on researching potential purchases and seeking validation that the products considered are appropriate for your unique learning needs and your student population. Then we discussed examples of technology integration into the components of your fail-safe literacy system. There are more possibilities than we could mention, but we attempted to provide examples that will assist you in thinking of a system, rather than of individual technology acquisitions. Acquisition is not the answer to student achievement—the answer is appropriate technology integration, with commensurate professional development and evaluation of effectiveness, then kicking it up a notch each year for continuous progress in creating joyful, independent readers, writers, and content learners.

HELPFUL TERMS

21st-century skills: Skills our students will need to be productive members of society.

Curriculum integration: The effective integration of technology throughout the curriculum to help students meet standards.

Electronic books (e-books): Books that can be downloaded.

E-book reader (e-reader): The application used to view e-books, with enhancements such as music, simulation, and sound effects.

Hypertext: Text that, when clicked on, opens other texts, making the content nonlinear.

Handhelds: Mobile, wireless devices or computers that fit into the palm of your hand.

Information literacy: Knowing how to locate, analyze, and use information to create authentic learning experiences and projects.

International Society for Technology in Education (ISTE): Nonprofit professional organization with worldwide membership of leaders of instructional and educational technology.

Personal digital assistant (PDA): Mobile electronic device that contains personal organizer functions such as a calendar and an address book, as well as applications for teaching and learning.

Technology integration: Infusion of technologies, such as hardware and software, into subject-specific content, to enhance learning and achieve standards.

Technology Standards for School Administrators (TSSA): Technology standards and skills identified as the foundation of what administrators of prekindergarten–twelfth grades must possess.

Video streaming: Simultaneously downloading and viewing video over the Internet.

FURTHER READING AND RESOURCES

Figure 6.1 Helpful Web Sites

Name and URL	*Description*
AlphaSmart, Inc www.alphasmart.com	A technology provider for classroom solutions, focused on reducing the cost and complexity of computing.
Florida Online Reading Professional Development (FORPD) www.itrc.ucf.edu/forpd	FORPD is a project funded by the Florida Department of Education to provide online staff development intended to help teachers improve reading instruction for learners in grades pre-K–12.
Forum Unified Education Technology Suit ences.ed.gov/pubs2005/tech_suite/	A practical guide that provides tested approaches to obtaining, managing, and integrating technology in various educational environments.
K-12 Handhelds www.k12handhelds.com/	Providing resources for administrators, teachers, and all educators is the focus of this site.
Media Centers for Literacy www.sunlink.ucf.edu/makingthe grade/summary.pdf	An abbreviated version of *Making the Grade: The Status of School Library Media Centers in the Sunshine State and How They Contribute to Student Achievement* is offered here.
Factors that Affect the Effective Use of Technology for Teaching and Learning www.seirtec.org/publications/lesso ndoc.html	Super resources provided by the Southeast Initiatives Regional Technology in Education Consortium concerning professional development for educators.
Starfall.com www.starfall.com/	This is a super Web site, created to assist young students in learning to read. You will find online stories, movies, and games that all promote the five constructs of literacy.
The WebQuest Place webquest.sdsu.edu/	This site provides information about, training for, and examples of this useful tool.

Blasewitz, M., & Taylor, R. (1999, January). Attacking literacy with technology in an urban setting. *Middle School Journal*, *30*(3), 33–39.

Gunter, G. A. (2001). Making a difference: Using emerging technologies and teaching strategies to restructure an undergraduate technology course for preservice teachers. *Education Media International*, *38*(1), 13–20.

Gunter, G. A., & Baumbach, D. (2003, December). Curriculum integration. In A. Kovalchick & K. Dawson (Eds.), *Educational innovation and reform: An encyclopedia of instructional technologies*. Santa Barbara, CA: ABC-CLIO.

Hasselbring, T. S., Goin, L., Bottge, B., Taylor, R., & Daley, P. (1997, November). The computer doesn't embarrass me. *Educational Leadership*, *55*(3), 30–33.

Microsoft. (2003). *Microsoft; Holt, Rinehart Winston; HP; and Orange County Public Schools collaborate on Tablet PC-based education project*. Retrieved January 28, 2005, from www.Microsoft.com/presspass/press/2003/aug03/08-22HoltHPTabletPR.asp

Mitchell, D., & Gunter, G. A. (2004). The TIME model: TIME to make a change to integrate technology. *Journal of Educational Media and Library Science*, *41*(4), 479–502.

National Association of Elementary School Principals & National Association of Secondary School Principals. (2003). *K–12 principals guide to no child left behind*. Arlington, VA: Educational Research Service. Retrieved January 28, 2005, from www.naesp.org/client_files/NCLB.pdf

North Central Regional Educational Laboratory. (2003). *enGauge 21st century skills: Literacy in the digital age 2003*. Retrieved February 7, 2005, from www.ncrel.org/engauge/skills/skills.htm

Shelly, G. A., Cashman, T. J., Gunter, R. E., & Gunter, G. A. (2004). *Teachers discovering computers: Integrating technology in the classroom* (3rd ed.). Boston: Course Technology.

Taylor, R. (2001, Fall). Teacher's challenge. *Journal of Staff Development*, *22*(4), 56–59.

Taylor, R. (2001, October). Steps to literacy. *Principal Leadership*, *2*(2), 33–38.

Taylor, R. (2002, September). Creating a system that gets results for the older, reluctant reader. *Phi Delta Kappan*, *84*(1), 85–88.

Taylor, R., Hasselbring, T. S., & Williams, R. D. (2001, October). Reading, writing and misbehavior. *Principal Leadership*, *2*(2), 33–38.

7 Completing the Fail-Safe System of Literacy

As a fail-safe literacy leader, you have created a system of literacy that is based on research on literacy learning and data related to your school and community. Faculty, staff, and administration have a clear understanding of exemplary literacy behavior and have committed to it. Roles and responsibilities related to literacy learning are noted and accepted. Action items are doable and realistic and will enhance student achievement. Finally, you have considered how you may enhance reading, writing, and content learning with technology integration. With all of this behind you and teachers on their way to improving learning, there remain four steps:

Step 8: Creating a support system

Step 9: Communicating the fail-safe literacy system

Step 10: Monitoring the fail-safe literacy system

Step 11: Celebrating successes

Many of these items or related items have surfaced during the planning process and need to be formalized. This is the time and place to do it.

STEP 8: CREATING A SUPPORT SYSTEM

Those working in schools today know that at this point, a generous amount of input has been processed, invited, and accepted. Once nonnegotiable expectations for daily practice, exemplars, roles and responsibilities, and doable action items have been generated that are a step ahead of many in the school and district, a support system to ensure smooth implementation, monitoring, and adjustment is recommended. *Support systems* refers to whatever it takes to make this fail-safe literacy system successful.

Professional development is one part of the support system. Previously, you noted action items for professional development that will assist you. Think through professional development again with the focus on nonnegotiables, exemplars, and roles and responsibilities. What do all stakeholders need to get started successfully? Figure 7.1, an example of professional development prioritizing, may be a tool that will assist you in determining where to begin. Select your nonnegotiables and exemplars as the items to be rated. If you are enhancing literacy learning with technology integration, related professional development should be included. The point is to align professional development with your literacy system.

Figure 7.2, an example of a professional development action plan, may also be helpful in conceptualizing a targeted plan for the year. For instance, you can see that there are a variety of professional development experiences included, all focused on the nonnegotiables and exemplars. Every item is not a workshop, but all items relate to each other.

When *Just Read, Lake!* was being developed, it became apparent that school-based, consistent, professional development across the district was critical to smooth implementation. That is why the budgeting priority for literacy coaches was noted. Following identification of the priorities for professional development, the literacy coaches created a series of eight *Just Read, Lake!* professional development modules, with a consistent research-base, for pre-kindergarten through Grade 12. These modules are delivered within the school day or afterwards, depending on the choice of the teachers. Additionally, an in-depth analysis of the current district professional development was conducted to determine which of the reading components for which grade levels were offered. Gaps were identified, and plans were made to eliminate gaps in district offerings.

Other components of a support system may include an instructional plan guide for administrators and teachers. A template for

Figure 7.1 Prioritization of Professional Development: Example

Directions: All of the items listed here are important in creating a fail-safe system of literacy. Prioritizing professional development in these subjects provides guidance for funding and scheduling. For each item, rate the need for professional development from 5 to 1, with 5 being the highest priority.

Component	*Rating (High) 5 → 1 (Low)*	*Comments*
Creating a print-rich environment		
Developing instructional plans using the processes of literacy		
Reading to and with students		
Using fiction and nonfiction to teach vocabulary, content		
Motivating accountable independent reading		
Developing fluency in content classes		
Using multiple symbol systems to teach vocabulary		
Using language literacy in mathematics		
Teaching, modeling, and practicing strategies of expert readers		
Developing instructional plans, using before, during, and after reading strategies		

instructional planning is found in Figure 7.3. This template can be modified for any district's or school's unique requirements. Note that the nonnegotiable expectations for daily practice are at the top, and the plan is divided into before reading, during reading, and after reading to encourage teachers to plan accordingly. This template is consistent with the daily nonnegotiables and assists teachers in achieving the expectations created in the fail-safe literacy system. This consistency will assist teachers in planning until automaticity develops.

Figure 7.2 Professional Development Action Plan: Example

Participants	*Component*	*When*	*Fiscal Impact*	*Results*
Whole staff	Awareness session	Preplanning	None	Feedback
Language Arts	Study group: *It's Never Too Late* (Allen, 1995) *Teaching Young Adult Literature* (Brown & Stephens, 1995)	August–November January–May	$150 $150	Classroom changes, student grades, teacher feedback
Language Arts	Monthly strategy sessions	Wednesday during planning period	$100 District and publisher consultant	Lesson plans, observations
Reading	Study group: *There's Room for Me Here* (Allen & Gonzalez, 1998)	August–November, after school	$100	Lesson plans, observations
Language Arts and Reading	Accountable independent reading strategies	September 8	$2000 for substitute teachers, consultant	Number of books read
Content areas	Strategy series: *A Handbook of Content Literacy Strategies* (Stephens & Brown, 2000)	September–May Fourth Wednesday during planning period	$300	Lesson plans, observation, feedback, participation
Administrators	Attend sessions and participate in study groups	August–May	None	Pre–post knowledge, coaching
Whole faculty	Online courses	August–May	TBD District purchase?	Feedback, completion of courses
Selected faculty	Conference attendance	August–May	$5000	Presentations to faculty, instructional changes

Note: TBD indicates "to be determined."

Figure 7.3 Fail-Safe Literacy Instructional Plan Template

All fail-safe literacy instructional plans incorporate the daily nonnegotiables: • Use literacy processes (reading, writing, speaking, listening, viewing, thinking, and expression through multiple symbol systems). • Read to and with students to provide access to on-grade-level content. • Teach and model strategies of expert readers before, during, and after reading.	
Subject or class:	Teacher:
Dates:	
Standards, benchmarks, or grade-level equivalents:	
Instructional materials and technology:	
Before reading: [access prior knowledge and provide base of knowledge]	
During reading: [enhance comprehension, thinking, vocabulary, connections]	
After reading: [enhance comprehension; move to long-term memory; connect to self, other texts, outside world, and next unit]	

A related support for teachers was developed at Umatilla Middle School. The literacy coach gave each administrator and teacher a 3 × 5 card with the daily non-negotiables and six key comprehension strategies on it. This is a handy, ready reference, and everyone is implementing the expectations.

Classroom literacy guides or rubrics will provide value in creating consistency. These guides are not evaluations but self-reflection tools, related to improving reading, writing, and content learning, which are consistent with nonnegotiable expectations for daily practice, exemplars, and roles and responsibilities. Figure 7.4 is a classroom guide and Figure 7.5 is a leadership guide. Both of these were developed to assist teachers and administrators with consistency and are included in *Just Read, Lake!* At South Lake High School, the literacy coach and administrators modified the classroom guide to include space for notation of dates of walk-throughs and comments. This is effective, as the coach and administrators are in classes every day but meet formally with teachers only about every nine weeks. Having these notations assists the administrator in commending the teachers and in coaching them. Sebastian River High School has adopted and modified the South Lake High School guide. Sebastian River finds the new walk-through guide to be helpful, as it focuses the daily work of instructional leadership, which can easily be derailed with crises and management issues.

STEP 9: COMMUNICATING OF THE FAIL-SAFE LITERACY SYSTEM

Developing a sequential roll-out of the fail-safe literacy system is a good idea. Think about all of the stakeholders with whom you should communicate. If this is a district system, the superintendent will want to present the system and the process to the board of education, to all principals, to parent leadership councils, and perhaps to the media. Essential items for principals to communicate to their faculty and staff include a consistent plan, expectations, and the support system.

Pam Saylor, the superintendent in Lake County, Florida, created a CD and script for her presentation to the school board and to all constituent groups. Principals then used the same presentation to share the literacy system with their faculties during the planning days before school opening. This well-planned roll-out provided the groundwork for the professional development and support that followed.

If you are a principal, make your fail-safe literacy system come alive with your personal participation, energy, and leadership.

Figure 7.4 Classroom Guide for Literacy, PreK-12

Self-monitoring will help identify areas for growth and celebration. You may use this form for self-assessment and for making your professional development plan. Also, you may want to ask for input from colleagues. Check the box for each line that best represents your classroom.

	N	*P*	*RM*	*Action Plan*
The classroom has:				
Literacy-rich and print-rich environment				
Differentiated instruction or stations				
Attractive, risk-free environment				
Smooth schedule, groups, transitions				
Student-known routines, resources				
Maximized time for literacy learning				
Integration of literacy content with standards				
Celebration of learning				
The teacher:				
Incorporates the seven processes of literacy				
Incorporates critical thinking strategies				
Models joy of reading to and with students daily				
Provides daily accountable independent reading for K–5 and 6–12 below-grade-level readers				
Assists students in selecting reading materials				
Promotes reading of nonfiction				
Monitors reading improvement with student data				
Teaches, models, and practices before, during, and after literacy strategies				

Note: N indicates novice; P, proficient; RM, role model.

Figure 7.5 Literacy Leadership Guide for PreK-12

Self-monitoring will help identify areas for growth and celebration. You may use this form for self-assessment and for making professional development plans. Also, you may want to ask for input from colleagues. Place a check in the box that best represents you.

Literacy Leadership	*N*	*P*	*RM*	*Action Plan*
Creates expectations across all content areas				
Analyzes and organizes student data				
Takes action on student achievement data				
Ensures a systematic process of professional development that includes opportunities, participation, and follow-up				
Participates in professional development with teachers				
Monitors instruction and provides feedback; visits classrooms daily and coaches teachers				
Develops intervention programs and monitors student growth				
Prioritizes appropriate personnel, materials, technology, schedule, use of time for students reading below grade level				
Leads a school literacy leadership team in development and implementation of literacy system				
Creates aligned curriculum, instruction, materials, and technology				
Engages parents and community in literacy learning				
Leads the selection of and monitors use of appropriate scientific, research-based student materials and technology				

Note: N indicates novice; P, proficient; RM, role model.

Develop a sequential communication of the system and its daily influence on teaching and learning. Communicating clearly with those to whom you report will assist you in accessing resources needed to maximize success in student achievement. Remember that the components addressed in Chapter 5 are those needed to fulfill NCLB plans and will be helpful in securing grants. Parents, teachers, students, and community members should have explicit information regarding your fail-safe literacy system. Think about posting it on the school or district's Web site, as well as providing updates and successes in a regular e-mail communications. This will empower stakeholders to fulfill their roles as expected and support the students.

STEP 10: MONITORING THE FAIL-SAFE LITERACY SYSTEM

Right now, before the implementation, decide what the monitoring system will be and who will conduct it. Stakeholders should know from the beginning how success will be determined. The process should not be cumbersome but be a view of what is improving and what is not improving that is easy to determine. Monitoring of the fail-safe literacy system should be an ongoing process, not one that waits until annual test data is returned. Determine your monitoring process based on the same data you used to identify needs: student achievement (by subgroups), student attendance, teacher attendance, and so on. You will also look at teacher grade profiles, and perhaps student grade point averages, or numbers of students in higher level courses, or satisfactory performance on advanced placement exams. Have the data changed that you looked at to determine your needs? When you make a graph of the data, do they show a positive trend?

Another way to consider the monitoring process of the fail-safe literacy system is in relationship to teacher and administrator behaviors. Teacher behavior changes long before you can measure growth in student achievement on a standards-based exam. How many are consistently using the nonnegotiables and exemplars? How close are you to regularly fulfilling your literacy roles and responsibilities? Have any of your exemplars become standard practice? How about professional development attendance and linking to classroom practice? These are the types of items we included in the first- and second-year evaluation of implementation of *Just Read, Lake!* in addition to literacy achievement data. In fact, 98% of all teachers in the district attended the Essential Core

Professional Development Module workshops, and schools report that the culture of literacy in the schools has changed and student achievement is moving in a positive direction. More change has been noted at the middle and high school levels than at the elementary levels, which can be expected.

In visiting classrooms and media centers, I see teachers creating print-rich environments, reading to students and incorporating content-related fiction and nonfiction and accountable independent reading, long before formal assessment data shows results. Within this book, you have been given examples of teachers engaging in new practices and of media specialists energizing media centers and making them more student friendly. These positive changes should be noted and celebrated every time they are observed. As you develop the monitoring process, make it as close to the classroom or daily practice as possible. The fail-safe literacy system is intended to be teaching and learning focused, so *that* is where you should target the monitoring process.

STEP 11: CELEBRATING SUCCESSES

Without a doubt, you will find multileveled successes. So, right in that evaluation plan, include a celebration. When the Sebastian River High School literacy system was being developed, the teachers wrote right in the document that they would have an Outback Restaurant night! There will be much to celebrate as teachers are more successful and students become better readers, writers, and content learners.

CONTINUING TO KICK IT UP A NOTCH

Are we there yet? Just when you are celebrating, you think, "What do we do now?" A healthy system feeds on itself and is always improving. As you look over the growth and positive changes that have taken place, you will want to take some time with your LLT or faculty to revisit the fail-safe literacy system planning process.

Bring out those exemplars and review them. After a year, which ones have become status quo and thus need to be moved to the right, becoming nonexemplars? What will the new exemplars be? Some exemplars may need to remain as such for another year if they are not being consistently implemented. Revisiting and revising exemplars will kick learning up another notch.

Ask again, "What is working in literacy learning and what is not?" Use the same categories as you did the year before. Some action items worked well, and some need a review or revision. As the second year ensued for the fail-safe literacy system at Sebastian River High School, assistant principal Joe Mills recognized that the vocational teachers were essential to improving reading and writing but that they were having difficulty teaching the vocabulary and content. He searched for vocationally related materials to share with those staff members, to assist them in developing better readers and writers. Again, refinements will be needed, but there will be much to celebrate. Are there budgetary items that are needed or priorities to be set?

As the teachers and students become more literacy savvy, they will want to continue to sharpen their skills, particularly if they are empowered and reinforced for doing so. Do not forget to plan for bringing new teachers or administrators up to speed on the fail-safe literacy system. For schools that are growing rapidly or have turnover in faculty, this is a critical component for continuous improvement.

REVIEW AND REFLECTION

Fail-safe literacy leadership and development of a fail-safe literacy system is predicated upon belief in the concepts of instructional leadership, accountability, and research on literacy learning. Over time, as I visit schools implementing these concepts, I see change. When I entered Jackson Heights Middle School in Seminole County, Florida, during its second year of professional development, I was struck with the changes. The hallways were full of photos of the principal and significant school personnel reading, with the caption "Reading by Example." On entering the media center, I saw walls of Your Recommended Books and Your Favorite Reads. Parent volunteers were transforming the media center into a forest to celebrate reading *Hoot* by Carl Hiaasen (2002). The media specialist had surveyed the students about their favorite "reads" and books they would recommend and made wall-size displays of both. Outside a classroom was a huge vocabulary wall of words, followed by visual displays of the definitions. These are exemplars for that school.

This is just one example of observing literacy learning changes. Observation starts with the leadership, as it did at Jackson Heights, but it has to include all faculty for all students to be touched by literacy infusion. This is fail-safe literacy, in which all students become better readers, writers, and content learners.

HELPFUL TERMS

Classroom guide: Template for reflection on professional behavior for literacy learning.

Leadership guide: Template for reflection on professional behavior as a literacy leader.

FURTHER READING AND RESOURCES

Hiaasen, C. (2002). *Hoot*. New York: Knopf.

Appendix A

APEL Template
Accountability Practices of Educational Leaders

Accountability Practices of Educational Leaders (APEL)

Please respond to the following statements by indicating to what extent each of these conditions applies to your school. Do not evaluate the conditions in terms of good or bad but only in terms of whether they take place in your school. Mark each item with one checkmark in the appropriate column. Please also complete the demographic information at the end of this survey.	**Strongly Agree**	**Mildly Agree**	**Mildly Disagree**	**Strongly Disagree**
Data-Driven Decision Making				
1. Standardized test data are analyzed, disseminated, and explained to all faculty. 2. Student achievement data (other than test results) are analyzed, disseminated, and explained to all faculty. 3. Instructional practices are consistent with research. 4. Opportunity to "benchmark" against best practices is possible (visiting other teachers to determine what works in that setting.) 5. All facets of the school's operation are open to change through data examination. 6. Evaluation and assessment of programs and processes are ongoing. 7. Data are collected and analyzed before decisions are made. 8. Climate Survey data are collected regularly from staff. 9. Climate Survey data are collected regularly from parents. 10. Training sessions are provided to parents to help them understand school data and how they relate to state policies.				

Continuous Improvement	Strongly Agree	Mildly Agree	Mildly Disagree	Strongly Disagree
1. The school's strengths have been identified and communicated to staff, students, and parents.				
2. New teams or committees are formed as new issues and concerns are identified.				
3. Continuous professional learning is highly valued by teachers at this school.				
4. Teachers adjust their teaching techniques based on student achievement.				
5. The solution to problems often raises additional issues that are also resolved.				
6. Teachers discuss student achievement issues in grade level meetings on a regular basis.				
7. Continued expansion of shared decision making is particularly important at this school.				
8. Schedules are continuously evaluated in order to find more time for academics.				
9. Grade level teams meet at least monthly to evaluate their progress toward school goals.				
10. A shared vision with clear goals that focus on increasing student achievement has been established for this school.				

Please respond to the following statements by indicating to what extent each of these conditions applies to your school. Do not evaluate the conditions in terms of good or bad but only in terms of whether they take place in your school. Mark each item with one checkmark in the appropriate column. Please also complete the demographic information at the end of this survey.	**Strongly Agree**	**Mildly Agree**	**Mildly Disagree**	**Strongly Disagree**
Shared Curriculam Focus on Standards				
1. Students not achieving standards are always provided with extra help. 2. Teachers implement specific strategies designed to help students see value in achieving standards. 3. This staff truly believes that all students can achieve high standards. 4. Teachers choose instructional materials specifically to support standards instruction. 5. This school has an ongoing student recognition program for standards achievement. 6. Teachers adjust their teaching techniques based on student progress toward benchmarks and standards. 7. Teams spend time discussing how to improve student progress toward benchmarks and standards. 8. Most teachers provide ample opportunity for students to experience success on standards. 9. Teams meet regularly to work on aligning curriculum with state standards. 10. Most teachers involve their students in setting personal goals to achieve standards.				

Leadership for Change and Innovation	Strongly Agree	Mildly Agree	Mildly Disagree	Strongly Disagree
1. Teams of teachers are often convened to solve school problems. 2. Collective professional growth is encouraged through grade level team meetings. 3. The leadership team (principal, asst. principal, counselor, etc.) researches and distributes information regarding best practices. 4. Teachers feel free to try innovative practices. 5. The school has a systematic procedure for recognizing staff achievement. 6. Professional development training is geared to needs identified by the staff. 7. The leadership team (principal, asst. principal, counselor, etc.) helps identify, break down, and eliminate barriers to change. 8. The leadership team (principal, asst. principal, counselor, etc.) focuses on instructional leadership above all else. 9. This school aims to achieve at least one standards-focused goal that can be accomplished in one year or less. 10. A strong professional learning community exits at this school. Years at current school: _____ Age: 21–25, 26–30, 31–35, 36–40, 41–45, 46–50, 51–55, 56–60, 61–65 Years as a principal: _____ Highest degree earned: _____ Free and reduced lunch percentage at your school: _____				

Reprinted from The *Relationship of Accountability Practices of Elementary Principals to Student Achievement,* by Dr. Carol Chanter (2002). Used with permission of Dr. Carol Chanter.

Appendix B

The Fail-Safe Literacy System Planning Process

Improvement in reading and writing and standards-based content learning takes a commitment on the part of the whole school. With the support of a literacy leadership team representative of the professional staff, cultural change will emerge. Everyone may not get on board at first, but with the same, consistent message being sent by key people, literacy infusion will be part of the culture of the school after a while. In this appendix are steps to follow to ensure your success. The process is exciting and will move smoothly when there is good planning.

Step 1: Commit to all students being joyful, independent readers and writers with equal access to the standards-based curriculum.

A. Develop a timeline and events for the development of the fail-safe literacy system.

B. Study proven and promising practices that are research-based and that combine literacy development and student development. Examples follow.

   1. Teachers develop instructional plans that incorporate the processes of literacy: reading, writing, speaking, listening, and viewing.

   2. Students read independently with accountability on a daily basis.

   3. Phonics and phonemic awareness instruction is included for primary grade students. Most middle and high school students can decode. Those who cannot will receive

immediate intervention from a reading teacher who understands decoding.

4. All teachers teach, model, and practice before reading, during reading, and after reading strategies to maximize comprehension and success.
5. Students reread passages for different purposes and at different times to reach deeper levels of understanding. Rereading develops fluency.
6. Direct instruction, practice, and integration of content and processes is provided. Teachers who do all of these achieve the highest student achievement; teachers who do only one or two have lower achievement.
7. Teachers integrate writing with reading. Reading and writing improve together.
8. Classrooms have a variety of reading materials. Reading levels, subjects, and genres vary to meet the instructional level, independent reading level, and interests of all of the students. Interesting nonfiction is available in the classroom. At least 50% of the print in the classroom is nonfiction.
9. Teachers read aloud to give students access to on-grade-level text, to model the joy of reading, and to model strategies that good readers use. *Read-alouds* are when the teacher reads and students listen.
10. Teachers incorporate shared reading to develop comprehension, interest, and vocabulary. *Shared reading* is when the teacher reads aloud and students follow along. It can give students access to texts that they would not otherwise have.
11. Conventions of grammar are taught in the context of reading and writing.
12. Test-taking skills are integrated into the daily work of students.
13. Teachers use guided reading and writing to work with small groups with similar reading levels.

What other proven and promising practices would you consider implementing?

Step 2: Based on the research, define *literacy*. This definition will guide the rest of the process and should drive instruction.

Step 3: Based on the research, determine the daily nonnegotiables that your team will commit to.

Step 4: Develop exemplars and nonexemplars for

A. Reading, language arts and English, content classes, vocational, physical education, electives, media center, second language, special education, and other areas.

Step 5: Define and commit to roles and responsibilities. Key players in improving literacy have defined roles.

A. Principal

B. Assistant principal

C. Dean

D. Resource specialist or literacy coach

E. Language arts teachers

F. Content area teachers

G. Media specialist

H. District personnel

Step 6: After reviewing data on student achievement, as well as other pertinent data, such as attendance of students and teachers, identify what is working and what is not working in literacy learning for students reading below grade level, at grade level, and above grade level.

A. English and language arts

B. Reading or intervention

C. Content areas

D. Vocational, arts, and electives

E. Media center

F. Before school

G. After school

H. Summer school

I. Parents and community

How will you improve what is not working and reinforce and expand on what is working? Are your curriculum, instruction, materials and technology, assessment, professional development, intervention, and parent and community aligned? Identify actions to take and unproductive practices to eliminate.

Action	*Who*	*When*	*Results*

Step 7: What else needs to take place for literacy learning to improve? What resources are needed to implement the plans you have identified?

Resources	*Budget Need*
Personnel	
Materials	
Time	
Equipment	

Step 8: What do you and your faculty need as a support system to ensure success?

A. Professional development
   1. English or language arts
   2. Reading or intervention
   3. Content areas
   4. Vocational, arts, and electives
   5. Media center
   6. Leadership

B. Classroom guides or rubrics

C. What else?

Step 9: Develop a communication and implementation timeline.

Step 10: Develop an evaluation of the fail-safe literacy system. How will you know that the system is working?

Step 11: How will you celebrate? Plan celebrations for along the way and critical times.

References

Allen, J. (1995). *It's never too late: Leading adolescents to lifelong literacy.* Portsmouth, NH: Heinemann.

Allen, J., & Gonzalez, K. (1998). *There's room for me here.* Portland, ME: Stenhouse.

Billmeyer, R., & Barton, M. L. (1998). *Teaching reading in the content areas: If not me, then who?* Aurora, CO: McREL.

Brown, J., & Stephens, E. (1995). *Teaching young adult literature.* New York: Wadsworth.

Burnett, L. (2004). *Visual literacy: Learn to see, see to learn.* Alexandria, VA: ASCD.

Chanter, C. L. (2002). *The relationship of the accountability practices of elementary school principals to student achievement.* Unpublished doctoral dissertation, University of Central Florida, Orlando.

Cupid-McCoy, J. P. (2003). *The relationship of accountability practices of middle school principals and FCAT reading achievement.* Unpublished doctoral dissertation, University of Central Florida, Orlando.

Dodge, B. (1997). *Some thoughts about WebQuests.* Retrieved February 7, 2005, from edweb.sdsu.edu/courses/edtec596/about_webquests.html

Doman, J. R. (1984). Learning problems and attention deficits. *Journal of the National Academy for Child Development, 4*(6), 8.

Domine, V. (2002). "We're wired! Now what?" A holistic approach to technology planning in high schools. *Journal of Literacy and Technology, 2*(2). Retrieved December 15, 2003, from www.literacyandtechnology.org/v2n2/domine/domine.htm

Gunter, G. A., & Murphy, D. (1997). Technology integration: The importance of administrative support. *Education Media International, 34*(3), 136–139.

Gunter, G. A., & Sivo, S. (2003). Effective online training: the Georgia GET FIT initiative. In *Technology and Teacher Education Annual: 2003.* Charlottsville, VA: Association for the Advance of Computing Education.

Harvey, S., & Goudvis, A. (2000). *Strategies that work.* Portland, ME: Stenhouse.

Hiassen, C. (2002). *Hoot.* New York: Knopf.

Just read, Lake! (2003). Taveres, FL: Lake County Schools.

Microsoft. (2003). *Microsoft; Holt, Rinehart Winston; HP; and Orange County Public Schools collaborate on tablet PC-based education project* (Press release). Retrieved February 7, 2005, from http://www.microsoft.com/presspass/press/2003/aug03/08-22HoltHPTabletPR.asp

Monsef, P. (2002). *Students find their voice through multimedia.* Retrieved February 14, 2004, from www.glef.org/php/article.php?id-Art_980&key=188

Murphy, J. (2004). *Leadership for literacy: Research-based practice, preK–3.* Thousand Oaks, CA: Corwin.

National Association of Elementary School Principals & National Association of Secondary School Principals. (2003). *K–12 principals guide to No Child Left Behind.* Arlington, VA: Educational Research Service. Retrieved January 28, 2005, from www.naesp.org/client_files/NCLB.pdf

National Center for Education Statistics. (2005). *Forum unified education technology suite.* Retrieved February 6, 2005, from nces.ed.gov/pubs2005/ tech_suite/

No Child Left Behind Act of 2001, 20 U.S.C. (2002) http://www.ed.gov/policy/elsec/leg/esea02/pg34.html

Nugent, G. C. (1982). Pictures, audio, and print: Symbolic representation and effect on learning. *Education Communications and Technology Journal, 30,* 163–174.

Partnership for 21st Century Skills. (2003). *Learning for the 21st century.* Retrieved January 31, 2005, from www.21stcenturyskills.org/downloads/P21_Report.pdf

Reed, R. (2001, August). Streaming technology: An effective tool for elearning experiences. *National Association of Media and Technology Centers' Bulletin,* pp. 1–3.

Regional Technology in Education Consortia. (1996). *Guiding questions for technology planning* (Version 1.0). Retrieved January 31, 2005, from www.ncrtec org/capacity/guidewww/gqhome.htm

Robb, L. (2002). *Reader's handbook.* Wilmington, MA: Great Source.

Roberts, O. (2004). *The relationship between high school principals as instructional leaders and students' academic achievement.* Unpublished doctoral dissertation, University of Central Florida, Orlando.

Rushkoff, D. (1996). *Playing the future.* New York: HarperCollins.

Sciencesaurus: A student handbook. (2002). Wilmington, MA: Great Source.

Shelly, G. A., Cashman, T. J., Gunter, R. E., & Gunter, G. A. (2004). *Teachers discovering computers: Integrating technology in the classroom* (3rd ed.). Boston: Course Technology.

Stephens, E. C., & Brown, J. E. (2000). *A handbook of content literacy strategies: 75 practical reading and writing ideas.* Norwood, MA: Christopher-Gordon.

Taylor, R. T. (2003). *Developing readers, writers, and content learners.* Unpublished paper, Galef Institute, Los Angeles.

Taylor, R. T. (2004, October 14). [Literacy Leadership Institute, Dallas]. Unpublished notes.

Taylor, R. T., & McAtee, R. (2003, March). Turning a new page to life and literacy. *Journal of Adolescent and Adult Literacy, 46*(6), 478–480.

Teale, W. H., Leu, D. J., Jr., Labbo, L. D., & Kinzer, C. (2002, April). The CTELL project: New ways technology can help educate tomorrow's reading teachers. *The Reading Teacher, 55*(7). Retrieved January 31, 2005, from http://www.readingonline.org/electronic/elec_index.asp?HREF=/electronic/RT/4–02_Column/index.html

United Learning. (2004). Using video to enhance instruction. *eSchool News, 7*(1), 21–26.

ADDITIONAL SOURCES

Allington, R. (Ed.). (1998). *Teaching struggling readers.* Newark, DE: International Reading Association.

Allington, R., & Cunningham, P. (1996). *Schools that work: Where all children read and write.* New York: Addison-Wesley.

Anderson, R., Wilson, P., & Fielding, L. (1988). Growth in reading and how children spend their time outside of school. *Reading Research Quarterly, 23,* 285–303.

Atwell, N. (1998). *In the middle: New understandings about writing, reading, and learning* (2nd ed.). Portsmouth, NH: Boynton/Cook.

Beers, K., & Samuels, B. (1998). *Into focus: Understanding and creating middle school readers.* Norwood, MA: Christopher-Gordon.

Calkins, L. (1994). *The art of teaching writing.* Portsmouth, NH: Heinemann.

CEO Forum on Education and Technology. (2001, June). *The CEO Forum school technology and readiness report: Key building blocks for student achievement in the 21st century: Assessment, alignment, accountability, access, analysis* (Year 4). Retrieved January 31, 2005, from ceoforum.org/downloads/report4.pdf

Cognition and Technology Group at Vanderbilt University. (1994). Multimedia environments for developing literacy in at-risk students. In B. Means (Ed.), *Technology and education reform: The reality behind the promise* (pp. 23–56). San Francisco: Jossey-Bass.

Educational Research Service. (2002). *Helping struggling readers at the elementary and secondary school levels.* Arlington, VA: Author.

Gambrell, L. B. (1996). Creating classroom cultures that foster reading motivation. *Reading Teacher, 50,* 1.

Hargreaves, A. (1997). *ASCD yearbook: Rethinking educational change with heart and mind.* Alexandria, VA: ASCD.

Harvey, S. (1998). *Non-fiction matters: Reading, writing and research in Grades 3–8.* Portland, ME: Stenhouse.

House, J. E., & Taylor, R. T. (2003, March). Leverage on learning. *Phi Delta Kappan, 84*(7), 537–540.

Jensen, E. (1998). *Teaching with the brain in mind.* Alexandria, VA: ASCD.

Joyce, B., & Showers, B. (1988). *Student achievement through staff development.* White Plains, NY: Longman Press.

Keene, E. O., & Zimmermann, S. (1997). *Mosaic of thought.* Portsmouth, NH: Heinemann.

Lambert, L. (1998). *Building leadership capacity in schools.* Alexandria, VA: ASCD.

Little, J. W. (1993, Summer). Teachers professional development in a climate of educational reform. *Educational Evaluation and Policy Analysis, 15*(2), 129–152.

Manning, T. (2000). *Achieving high quality reading and writing in an urban middle school: The case of Gail Slatko.* Retrieved January 31, 2005, from cela.albany.edu

Marsh, D. D. (1999). *ASCD yearbook: Preparing our schools for the 21st century.* Alexandria, VA: ASCD.

Marzano, R. J., Pickering, D. J., & Pollock, J. E. (2001). *Classroom instruction that works: Research-based strategies for increasing student achievement.* Alexandria, VA: ASCD.

Murphy, J. (2001, October 9). Leadership for literacy: Policy leverage points. Paper presented at the Educational Testing Service/Educational Commission of the States Conference on Leadership for Literacy, Washington, DC.

North Central Regional Educational Laboratory. (2003). *enGauge 21st century skills: Literacy in the digital age.* Retrieved January 31, 2005, from www.ncrel.org/engauge/skills/skills.htm

Patton, S., & Holmes, M. (1990). *The keys to literacy.* Washington, DC: Council for Basic Education.

Roach, R. (2002). Making the most of multimedia. *Black Issues in Higher Education, 19,* 47.

Romano, T. (1995). *Writing with passion: Life stories, multiple genres.* Portsmouth, NH: Heinemann.

Routman, R. (1994). *Invitations: changing teachers and learners K-12* (2nd ed.). Portsmouth, NH: Heinemann.

Smoker, M. (1996). *Results: The key to continuous school improvement.* Alexandria, VA: ASCD.

Smoker, M. (2001). *The results fieldbook.* Alexandria, VA: ASCD.

Snow, C., Burns, M. S., & Griffin, P. (1998). *Preventing reading difficulties in young children.* Washington, DC: National Academy Press.

Southeast Initiatives Regional Technology in Education Consortium. (2004). *The factors that affect the effective use of technology for teaching and learning.* Retrieved January 25, 2004, from www.seirtec.org/publications/lesson doc.html

Sprenger, M. (1999). *Learning and memory: The brain in action.* Alexandria, VA: ASCD.

Taylor, R. (1999, December). Missing pieces: aligned curriculum, instruction, and assessment. *Schools in the Middle, 9*(11), 14–16.

Taylor, R., Jones, P., & Mills, J. (2005, February). Fail-safe literacy. *Principal Leadership, 5*(6), 33-36.

Taylor, R., & Peterson, D. S. (2003, Winter). RISE: Service and learning combine. *Kappa Delta Pi Record, 39*(2), 70–73.

Togneri, W. (2003). *Beyond islands of excellence: What districts can do to improve instruction and achievement of all schools. A leadership brief.* Washington, DC: Learning First Alliance.

Tovani, C. (2000). *I read it, but I don't get it: Comprehension strategies for adolescent readers.* Portland, ME: Stenhouse.

Weaver, C. (1998). *Lessons to share on teaching grammar in context.* Portsmouth, NH: Heinemann.

Wilhelm, J. D. (2001). *Strategic reading guiding students to lifelong literacy: Grades 6–12.* Portsmouth, NH: Boynton/Cook.

Wolfe, P. (2001). *Brain matters.* Alexandria, VA: ASCD.

Index

The Corwin Press logo—a raven striding across an open book—represents the union of courage and learning. Corwin Press is committed to improving education for all learners by publishing books and other professional development resources for those serving the field of K–12 education. By providing practical, hands-on materials, Corwin Press continues to carry out the promise of its motto: **"Helping Educators Do Their Work Better."**